Meditating with Koans

D1500675

J. C. Cleary

Asian Humanities Press
Berkeley, California

ASIAN HUMANITIES PRESS

Asian Humanities Press offers to the specialist and the general reader alike, the best in new translations of major works and significant original contributions, to enhance our understanding of Asian literature, religions, cultures and thought.

Library of Congress Cataloging-in-Publication Data

Chu-hung, 1535-1615.
    [Ch'an kuan ts'e chin. English]
    Meditating with koans / [translated by] J. C. Cleary.
        p.   cm.
    Includes bibliographical references.
    ISBN 0-89581-902-3 : $10.00
    1. Meditation—Zen Buddhism—Early works to 1800.
2. Koan—Early works to 1800. I. Cleary, J. C. (Jonathan Christopher) II. Title.
BQ9288.C4813   1992
294.3'443—dc20
                                     92-19602
                                       CIP

Acknowledgements

This book is dedicated to my wife Mai and my friends Greg Gargarian, Jacqueline Karaaslanian, Howard Austin, Linda Mason, Byron Coffin, and Margaret Gargarian, and to Anna, Markie, and Georgie; and to my companions in Buddhism Thomas Cleary, Nguyen Tu Cuong, Lee Jinwol, Thich Thong Hai, and Qin Wenjie.

J.C.C.

Leap Year Day 1992

Contents

Introduction

1: Buddhism and Zen Buddhism

Meditating with koans was one of the methods employed in the Zen schools of East Asian Buddhism. The work translated below is a compendium of classic lessons from eminent Zen teachers on how to use koans to advance in the Buddhist Path.

The word "koan" seems to be gradually becoming naturalized in the English language, as information about the Zen school and its characteristic teaching styles and methods becomes more widely available in the West. But just as Zen itself has been enveloped in a cloud of misperceptions and misleading images, the Zen koan has remained a rather mysterious subject, and the practical nature and operational logic of Zen koans has been obscured.

What *are* koans? What is Zen itself for that matter?

Zen was part and parcel of what is called Mahayana, or "Great Vehicle" Buddhism. Zen arose as a movement with East Asian Buddhism dedicated to moving the lessons of the Buddhist scriptures and philosophical writings back into the realm of everyday practical experience after they had become objects of mere emotional veneration and intellectual appreciation in the Buddhist communities. The Zen adepts pointed out that the symbolic scenes and abstract concepts contained in the Buddhist scriptures and philosophical writings referred to states of the human mind. They emphasized that the scriptural and philosophical teachings mapped out a practical path to an all-encompassing mode of direct perception accessible to properly prepared human beings.

This direct perception of reality is what is called "enlightenment." According to the Buddhist teaching, all human beings are innately endowed with a potential for objective wisdom and unselfish compassion–this potential is called our buddha-nature. We are all potentially buddhas, all potentially enlightened, but in practice few of us fully realize this potential. Anyone who does manage to get in touch with his or her buddha-nature and gains the practical use of it is a *buddha*, an "enlightened one."

From this perspective, then, the historical founder of the Buddhist religion, the Indian sage who lived twenty-five hundred years ago variously called Gotama, Siddhartha, and Shakyamuni Buddha, was just one of the countless enlightened ones of the past, present, and future. Buddhists venerate Shakyamuni Buddha as a great exemplar of wisdom and compassion, but the message emphasized by the Zen school is that all of us have the potential to become enlightened, and that all Buddhists should aspire to reach the level of enlightenment epitomized by the Buddha himself. By following the Path of enlightenment to its culmination, we are simply realizing our true nature.

Buddhism has taken on a wide variety of forms over the course of its twenty-five hundred year history in Asia and elsewhere. From the Buddhist point of view, the particular way the Buddha Dharma (that is, the teaching of enlightenment) is expressed must be adapted to the particular mentality and outlook of the people to whom it is addressed, and this varies with the time and place. In essence, Buddhism is a formless teaching. There is no set doctrine or dogma, no inflexible routines or invariable methods. The Buddha Dharma is expressed in specific forms in order to communicate with the people of specific times and places.

The task of Buddhist teachers down through the ages has been to make a living adaptation of the Buddha Dharma that meets the needs of the people of the time and place in which the teachers happen to be operating. The guiding observation is that Reality itself in its totality is beyond the range of language and conventional categories. The only alternative for enlightened teachers is to devise methods and perspectives that serve the instrumental purpose of gradually preparing learners to experience more and more complete perceptions of reality. All the particular forms established as part of the Buddhist teaching–stories, conceptual schemata, community groupings, rituals, images, disciplinary practices, meditation techniques, and all the rest–have been intended as practical tools to help enable learners to unfold their potential for enlightened perception. This applies to koans and to all the other diverse methods of the Zen schools as well.

The criterion for genuineness in the Buddhist teaching is *effectiveness*. That is, real effectiveness in freeing people from their conditioning and opening the way for them to gain the use of their buddha-nature. The enlightening effectiveness of particular methods does not reside so much in the methods themselves, as in their proper use by clear-eyed expert teachers. To be effective, a given method must be employed with the right people at the right time in the right place. The expertise of the enlightened teachers who have upheld the Buddha Dharma lies precisely in their ability to make all these necessary judgments accurately.

Buddhist methods are traditionally compared to medicines, and Buddhist teachers to skilled physicians, who are able to diagnose the learners' mental states accurately and prescribe in a timely way the particular methods that will effectively transform them and unlock their enlightened potential.

Buddhist theory has always recognized that a conceptual schema or practical technique that may be valid or true in some abstract sense can be rendered ineffective and even counterproductive when misapplied. In Zen terminology, what were originally "living methods" turn into "dead methods" in the wrong hands. Even the most excellent and beautiful Buddhist teachings can become useless or worse when they are applied blindly without insight, misused through rote imitation, or made objects of emotional allegiance and sectarian dogmatism.

This process of degeneration of originally enlightening techniques in the hands of blind imitators is a well-known phenomenon throughout Buddhist history. The formless, infinitely adaptable reality of the Buddha Dharma has often been lost sight of and been replaced by rigid institutions, cliched formulas, and empty routines.

Part of the role of the enlightened Buddhist teachers down through the generations has been to work to counteract this tendency, and make sure that genuinely effective forms of the teaching of enlightenment remain available to learners with the right aspirations. This accounts for the cycles of renovation and reformulation of Buddhism by its adepts that we can observe down through Buddhist history.

The emergence of Zen itself marks one of these cycles in East Asian Buddhism. Although we use the Japanese form of the word in English, what we call Zen emerged as a distinct style of Buddhism in China in the seventh and eighth centuries A.D., then spread to Korea and Vietnam in the ninth century, and only reached Japan in the twelfth century. (Based on the Sanskrit word *dhyana*, which means "meditation," the Chinese name for this current of Buddhism is *Chan*, the Korean is *Son*, the Vietnamese is *Thien*, and the Japanese is *Zen*. We go on using the Japanese form of the name because word of Zen first reached the modern West via Japan, and because the word "Zen" fits into the sound pattern of English better than any of the alternatives.)

Misled by stylistic differences, some modern commentators have failed to see the intrinsic connection between Zen Buddhism and the previous traditions of Mahayana Buddhism. Within the Zen tradition itself, inability to see the compatibility of Zen with the Buddhism of the Mahayana sutras and philosophical treatises was taken as a sign of the failure to understand *both* Zen *and* the wider Mahayana tradition. Since Truth itself is formless, and the means of communicating it are necessarily multiform, the people within the Zen tradition saw *intent* as the key issue. They knew that the Zen teaching continued the fundamental intent of all the buddhas, as explained in the Lotus Sutra, which is to open up people's enlightened perception.

At the conceptual level, Zen theory and practice is obviously rooted in the formulations of the Avatamsaka Sutra and certain other Mahayana scriptures, and of the Indian philosophical schools known as Madhyamika and Yogacara. Genuine Zen teachers through the ages were well versed in these other forms of Buddhism, and freely drew upon the analytic categories and practical techniques they provided.

In terms of its immediate historical antecedents in China, the early Zen teachers drew upon a wide range of Mahayana materials, and were particularly close to the Tiantai form of Chinese Buddhism, which itself was a synthesis of theoretical perspectives and practical techniques drawn from the full Mahayana heritage. Zen writings at times made use of Taoist terminology from the pre-existing Chinese religious culture, but this practice had already been followed by the early pioneers of Buddhism in China who regularly took over Taoist terms whose meanings paralleled the Buddhist message.

The initial impetus of Zen was to insist that the lessons contained in the Buddhist sutras and philosophical writings must be put into practice in the here and now. The early Zen teachers looked around and saw too many Buddhists who piously worshipped the scriptures as sacred texts, or studied Buddhist philosophy as a theoretical exercise, without dreaming of taking the Dharma's fundamental message to heart and attempting to live it.

It is important to remember that from its earliest days and all through its history, Zen Buddhism employed a wide range of Buddhist techniques of perfecting generosity, discipline, forbearance, energy focus, meditation, and transcendent wisdom. No one method was ideologically privileged or routinely applied in all situations. In particular cases, adept teachers prescribed certain techniques and not others as appropriate to their students' needs, to be sure. But dogmatic adherence to a limited repertoire of techniques was always taken as a sign of the deterioration of a school and incompetence on the part of its teachers. To be qualified to function as a genuine Zen teacher, a person needed not only a firm basis in enlightened perception, but a thorough mastery of the full range of practical techniques comprising the Buddha Dharma.

2: **Zen Buddhism and Koan Study**

The use of koans was one of the distinctive methods employed by various Zen schools. In modern parlance, koans were *interactive semantic devices*, designed to interact with the learner's mind and assist in the unlocking of the inherent human potential for enlightened awareness. Koan study in certain Zen schools played a key part in the long process through which people transformed their consciousness with the guidance of qualified teachers and gained the free use of their buddha-nature.

The word *koan* (again, the Japanese form of the original Chinese term *gong-an*) literally means "public case." At a certain point in the history of Zen in China, records of the sayings and doings of the earlier Zen masters began to be used as instructional materials and meditation themes. These stories and sayings thus became "public cases" that many Zen people studied and focused their attention on.

As time went on, layers of commentary built up around the most famous koans, as generations of Zen teachers added appreciatory verses, prose commentaries, introductory pointers, abrupt interjections, and other explanatory and provocatory material to the well-known koans. Noted Zen teachers assembled collections of koans, together with prose and verse commentaries, and some of these became famous "reference books" studied by many learners down through the centuries in the Zen communities.[1] In these collections the chosen koans are arranged so as to promote a progressively deeper and more comprehensive perception of the total Buddhist message.

The koans encode the total Buddhist project in an extremely concise and elegant fashion. They present a map of the Buddhist Path, a map that illustrates learners' states of minds, describes the nature of the teacher-learner interaction, assesses the various experiential states and stations along the Path, and points to the complex reality of the destination.

Those who are familiar with the branches of Buddhist theory that the Zen school drew on can readily decode the koans in terms drawn from Madhyamika and Yogacara philosophy, and the Mahayana sutras, especially the Flower Ornament Scripture.[2] The koans present the same Buddhist message, but in the form of teaching stories and short sayings rather than the detailed philosophical treatises or vast symbolic tableaux of the earlier Buddhist writings. Considered as intellectual creations, the Zen koans represent extremely concentrated, concise, and elegant epitomes of the classic lessons of Mahayana Buddhist thought.

The koans were intended as tools to refine the learner's mind, and must always be understood as such. They were practical tools, not theoretical statements or exercises in intellectual cleverness. It is not for me to describe here the way the koans were used in Zen practice: this subject is treated with the insight of a true teacher in the work translated below, Dharma Teacher Zhuhong's *Impetus to Advance in the Zen Gate*.

3: Zen Koans and the Irrationalist Fallacy

Koans have always exercised an intellectual fascination over those who come in contact with them. Some have found Zen koans intriguing, other found them annoying; some have found them profound and intellectually challenging, others have dismissed them as meaningless and absurd. In Old Asia, where the Zen school exerted a formidable intellectual and cultural force for a thousand years, many people on the periphery of Buddhism came into contact with koans and other Zen teaching words and responded to them as purely intellectual creations, conceptual playthings, aesthetic vignettes, jeux d'esprit.

Because of the particular historical moment and cultural circumstances in which Zen began to become known in the Western world, a host of related misconceptions have sprung up around Zen and the Zen koans. Since these fallacies in many cases still impede a clear intellectual understanding of what Zen is all about, it is worth knocking some of them down.

The overarching fallacy is that Zen teaching is anti-intellectual and anti-rational, and that the Zen koans epitomize this.

For many people in the West, of course, the alleged anti-rationalism of Zen (and of other branches of the imagined "wisdom of the East") has actually been a big part of their appeal. It is hardly surprising that many people who reject the claims of "Reason" would appear in a civilization that claims to be built on Reason yet has routinely produced such absurdities as mass impoverishment of its own lower classes, the alienation of its people from their work, their bodies, and their souls, the blind destruction of other cultures, economic depressions and the two World Wars, and the rape of the ecosystem. For more than a century now, refugees from the irrational "Reason" of the West have been flocking into various cultural and religious movements promising a variety of outlandish alternatives.

Many of the would-be interpreters of Zen and other

wisdom traditions to the West have been a part of this turn away from Reason. They have eagerly projected onto Zen their favorite alternatives to rationality: subjectivism, intuition, instinctive feeling, all sorts of emotionalism and irrationalism. To interpreters of this type, Zen koans just express the futility of reason and logic and the need to transcend rational thought. Certain "interpreters of Zen" have selectively highlighted those koans which seem to serve this interpretation, while studiously ignoring the hundreds of other koans that do not. They have succeeded to the extent that for many outsiders, the word "paradoxical" has become the primary association of the words "Zen" and "koan."

There is actually a double fallacy at work here.

First of all, it is a fallacy to accept the rationalist apologia for modern Western civilization at face value, and conclude that if that civilization is destructive or misguided, that Reason itself is to blame. Before people disillusioned with Western civilization go looking for an imagined alternative to reason in the "mystic East," they would do well to acquaint themselves with the many deep critiques of fragmentary instrumental "reason" that have been developed in the modern West. People eager to escape from the tyranny of scientism and technocracy should delve into the profound findings about the limits of the axiomatic method and the multiplicity of potential logics that have been developed by modern investigations into the foundations of mathematics and science.

The second fallacy is to imagine that Buddhism as a whole, or Zen Buddhism in particular, takes its stand with the irrationalists, intuitionists, and romantic emotionalists against the strictures of Reason. Buddhism does reject the inflated claims for Reason made by many branches of traditional Western thought, but not in the way that the irrationalists and romantics imagine.

In Buddhist theory, Reason is not the spark of the divine within us, or the royal road to truth. The way the Buddhist seers viewed it, our capacity for intellectual thought based on logical reasoning and conceptualizing and classifying phenomena is a basic human faculty comparable to our ability to see, hear, taste, smell, and touch. Properly used, reason is a valuable tool both in worldly and world-transcending pursuits.

The problem with reason, according to the Buddhist seers, is that it becomes trapped in a limited, arbitrary, conditioned view of the world. Reason becomes entangled with our conditioned biases, desires and aversions. It is limited by the categories we have been conditioned to accept by our linguistic and cultural communities, and our personal histories. This conditioned version of reason sets itself up as a tyrant, channeling our perception into limiting, preconceived categories and censoring all inputs from reality that would tend to reveal a bigger picture.

Buddhist seers did not accept the inflated claims of conditioned commonsense reason and verbal logic to be direct windows on reality. Buddhist analysis focuses on the psychological conditioning that shapes perception, creates commonsense reason, and makes it seem objectively true. On the other hand, Buddhist theory does not agree that the only alternative to what is presumed to be rationality is some sort of hazy, subjective, unverifiable intuition. The Buddhist adepts experimentally discovered, verified, and mapped out a form of perception that goes beyond the confines of conditioned commonsense reason, but is nonetheless precise, definite, and astoundingly effective.

Thus the practical task of Zen (and other forms of the Buddhist teaching) is not to abolish or destroy the intellectual faculty, but to free it from its conditioning, to purify it, and to allow it to function in an accurate, dispassionate way. Part of this process involves breaking the moment-to-moment tyranny of the conditioned intellect, and showing the contradictions and absurdities to which conditioned reason leads. Koans are one means among many used for this end.

But the goal of Zen is not some blanked-out, blissed-out state of intuitive grace that many of the modern romantic irrationalists imagine as synonymous with enlightenment. Rather, the enlightened wisdom which Buddhist teaching aims to activate includes the capacity for what is called "differentiating wisdom"–the ability to accurately perceive the workings of complex, interlocking webs of cause-and-effect, and to formulate effective strategies for accomplishing the teaching mission of the buddhas.

The cliche that Zen is anti-rational and anti-intellectual has pervaded discussions of Zen in the West, both among the admirers and the detractors of Zen. It is repeated endlessly in popular books purporting to explain Zen and in scholarly tomes on comparative religion and Asian religion. But it is completely at odds with the facts.

If Zen was anti-intellectual, how did it manage to make such a profound impact on the intellectual world of East Asia? How is it that in old East Asia even the intellectual enemies of Zen felt obliged to answer to its perspectives, and often found themselves unwittingly drawn onto its intellectual terrain? How is it that Zen influences radiated through East Asian philosophy, aesthetics, and literature? How is it that even a down-to-earth, worldly philosophy like Confucianism became permeated with Zen ideas and practices?[3]

Not only was Zen *not* anti-intellectual, it was actually the intellectual spearhead of Buddhism in East Asia. The craftsmen of the Zen schools in old East Asia were able to produce such a rich outpouring of arresting ideas, startling metaphors, and beautiful literary images that no honest intellectual in that culture-area could ignore them. Even today, Zen and the Zen koans continue to be able to fascinate people the world over who appreciate the subtle use of words and ideas to create multiple levels of meaning.

As a result of the prominence and persistence of cliches about Zen associated with the irrationalist fallacy, it seems necessary to present a checklist of what koans are not.

Paradox is not the defining feature of koans. There is no one typical form for a koan. A koan might consist of a saying, or a question, or a question and an answer, or a dialogue, or a story of an interchange between Zen people, or even a quotation from the Buddhist scriptures. The koans are many and various: when speaking of the whole legacy of koans, Zen people conventionally referred to "the seventeen hundred koans." In the Appendix at the end of this book the reader can find a selection of koans that gives some hint of the variety of the koan form.

Koans should not be understood as mere exercises in repartee, or egocentric contests for intellectual supremacy. In koans that follow a question-and-answer format or a story format, the "characters" are not to be taken as individual people, but as personifications of certain attitudes and states of mind. The koans present the abstract core of certain Buddhist observations about

358'
4254

the human condition and the states and stations of the Buddhist Path. To understand them as battles of wit between personal rivals is to trivialize them and overlook their basic intent.

Koans are not puzzles or riddles. There are many koans that are not in the form of questions at all, and many koans that do contain a question also supply an answer. Unlike puzzles and riddles, the koans do not have pat answers. When put to their proper use within genuine Zen schools, koans were not tests of verbal cleverness or quick wits. Zen teachers knew how to use koans to develop their students' level of insight. The student's response to the koan was a way for the teacher to gauge the student's inner state. The real "answer" to the koan is not a sentence or a gesture in response to the teacher's question, but the change in the learner's mental state brought about by working with the koan.

At a certain stage of the decline of Buddhism in Japan, so-called koan study became a routinized method of gaining certification within a rigidly institutionalized form of state-supervised "Zen." The real liberating use of koans has nothing in common with the ritualized teacher-student interview formats and concept of "passing koans" carried on like a form of mummery. This institutional deterioration of Zen in Japan led debunkers to come out with books that claimed to reveal "the right answers" to the koans–meaning the standardized answers that the inmates of these institutions holding the office of teacher would accept to pass the student. It is indeed appalling to find that this travesty of koan study is still being carried on in various imitation-Zen groups even today.

Koans are not playthings and koan study is not an idle pursuit of conceptual novelty, intellectual fascination, or a sense of bewilderment. The Zen teachers devised methods to prepare learners to move beyond limited views, and gradually reach a position to witness Truth. The koans are one manifestation of this mode of teaching. Meditation focused on koans is used to undermine deluded perception, by interrupting the internal dialogue that maintains it. The koans open glimpses of the buddhas' direct, comprehensive perception of reality as a whole.

Koans are not defined by their occasional violation of logic or use of paradox. They are complex semantic devices, designed to interact with our ordinary minds in various ways, leading eventually to the discovery and recovery of our buddha-nature.

Modern commentators who have overemphasized the role of paradox and apparently illogical statements in koans in effect imply that all the koans basically convey one and the same message: that words and logic cannot express the truth. If this were really the only message being communicated, why were there hundreds of koans, all different, and how and why did the Zen masters find so much to say about them? When we look at the classic koan collections, it is powerful testimony to the koans' semantic richness that each koan could stand at the center of an intricate web of comments and provoke generations of conceptual reflections and reactions.

In fact, while some koans employ paradox, most do not, so paradox can hardly be taken as a defining feature of koans. Likewise, though some koans defy commonsense logic, others employ it: they do not simply reject logic, but use it in order to invite us to observe its operations and limitations more rigorously than commonsense has time for.

After all, the Buddhist project does not rest on a simplistic dichotomy between rational and intuitive modes, where the former is to be abandoned and the latter embraced. Buddhist enlightenment retains rationality as a tool, cleansing it of the conditioning that previously subverted it. Enlightened wisdom rests on nonconceptual direct perception that has nothing in common with the fuzzy subjectivity commonly associated with intuition.

Koans do not have definitive "answers" at the conceptual level. They all contain many layers of meaning. At first they intrigue our intellects, and provoke our habitual response of trying to understand and make sense. In this way, they show us the workings of our conceptual minds, our habits of thought, our systems of categories and patterns of analysis–in short, the whole edifice of mental conditioning which our training has made us wrongly accept as an accurate reflection of reality We might say that koans set in motion trains of thought, and then derail them. By doing this they break the continuity of the internal dialogue that maintains our usual (false) sense of reality. They bring home to us the limitations of the whole enterprise of conditioned thought, its inability to arrive at the ultimate answers.

The persistence of the irrationalist fallacy in the Western understanding of Zen and Zen koans may owe something to the fact that this fallacy has been highly congenial both to certain would-be friends and to the avowed foes of Buddhism and of the "wisdom of the East" in general. The Western foes of "mysticism" can easily pick out a couple of examples from D.T. Suzuki or Alan Watts of supposedly illogical, paradoxical koans, and triumphantly conclude that Zen is a load of irrational rubbish. The Western fans of "the wisdom of the

East" can turn to the same sources for confirmation of their fantasy that "mysticism" offers a quick shortcut to a kind of "intuitive" and "supra-rational" wisdom that leaves room for all kinds of self-indulgent sentimentalism and complacency.

Poor old Zen, caricatured by would-be friend and foe alike. It is worth observing that the modern day misconceptions of Zen are nothing new. A similar range of misconceptions about Zen was also present in old China during the heyday of the Zen teaching there. The curmudgeons and the cultists of today had their counterparts five hundred and a thousand years ago.

The defenders of conventional orthodoxy in old China were outraged and repelled by the unconventional behavior and talk of the Zen masters. Ignoring the professed intent of the Buddhist tradition, they accused the Zen school of fostering moral laxity and social irresponsibility. These old-time enemies of Zen refused to delve far into Zen lore, fearing its seductive powers. They felt safer with an attitude of invincible ignorance. A similar attitude prevails today in many scholarly circles, where it is considered plausible to specialize in Chinese intellectual history while knowing nothing of Buddhism and Taoism, two of the three main streams of Chinese intellectual history.

Meanwhile, the libertines and avant-garde artists and writers of old China were excited and attracted by the unconventional behavior and talk of the Zen masters. They proceeded to imitate Zen styles, using their interest in Zen as a license to revel in their own subjectivity. They equated their own whimsical iconoclasm and self-indulgence with the spontaneity of the Zen adepts. They perused Zen literature picking out bits and pieces they could take out of context and misinterpret as

supporting their own ideas of self-assertion and free-
dom. This approach to Zen has been followed by the
modern adherents of "Beat Zen" who mix Zen ideas into
a melange of countercultural attitudes and lifestyles.

Throughout Zen history, the genuine proponents
of the Zen school were left fundamentally unperturbed
by both opponents and misguided adherents, with their
wild ideas of the Zen Path. With their knowledge of the
psychology of delusion, the adepts could anticipate
these trends, and take every possible measure to keep
these mistaken ideas of Zen from interfering with the
real work of the Zen school. The Zen adepts knew that
the Buddha Dharma itself, the teaching of truth by truth,
would always remain, regardless of the current reputa-
tion of Zen among the uninformed.

4: Koans and the Zen Path

Zhuhong and all the Zen masters he quotes in the
anthology translated below had a clear idea of the basic
guidelines of the Zen Path, and the place of particular
methods such as koan study in the total Buddhist
project. These basic guidelines underlie all these lessons on koan study, and provide the implicit practical/
theoretical framework. Since this set of guiding principles may not be quite so familiar today, it is fitting to
restate some of the fundamental Zen perspectives on the
Path explicitly for the modern audience.

The aim of the Buddhist Path is to enable people to
transform their existence through recognizing their
buddha-nature and bringing to life their potential for
nondualistic awareness and selfless compassion. Beyond the limited scope of our conditioned perception,
there is a wider reality with its own inherent structure

and norms which determine the imperatives of the Path and the transformative process.

A wide variety of techniques is used to advance on the Path. Learners must be guided on the Path by adepts who know the imperatives of the Path and can devise a particular course of study suited to the needs and mentality of the individual learner. Adept teachers are needed to monitor the learner's progress and prescribe exercises and practices to fit the learner's evolving situation.

The Path in the experiential sense consists of a succession of states through which the learner's potential gradually unfolds. None of these experiential states is the final destination: getting stuck at any intermediate level of "mystical experience," no matter how sublime and wondrous, blocks further progress. In the collection below, Zhuhong cites several personal accounts by Zen people of the long and winding paths by which their realization was gradually refined and deepened and led into qualitatively new levels of awareness.

Zhuhong quotes the words of Zen master Zhongfeng:

"You may go twenty or thirty years without opening up to enlightenment. . . . Work hard and don't give up. . . No matter whether it takes three lifetimes or five lifetimes or ten lifetimes or a hundred lifetimes, be sure not to stop until you have penetrated through to enlightenment. If you have a correct basis [in genuine aspiration and rightly guided practice], do not worry that you will not completely illuminate the great matter [of enlightenment]."

The Zen Path is not a matter of rote formulas, and it is not a case of "one size fits all." It takes supreme dedication and effort on the part of the learner, and an expert teacher to act as a guide. An expert teacher by definition is someone who has already travelled the Path to the end, and transcended the limits of egocentric, conditioned perception and the vagaries of personalistic motivations.

When modern people hear of the crucial role of enlightened teachers in directing the learner's progress on the Path, they often react with the natural practical question: Where can such teachers be found?

The classic answer may not be comforting, but it has truth on its side. According to the Buddhist teaching, Truth has an inherent justice and can only be experienced by those who seek Truth for its own sake. It cannot be communicated to the unqualified or denied to the qualified. The key variable is thus the genuineness of the learner's aspiration, and the purity of his or her motivations. Hence the classic answer to the question of how to link up with an enlightened teacher: They are ready when we are.

5: The Present Work

The original title of the anthology translated below is *Impetus to Advance in the Zen Gate* [Chan Men Ze Jin] This book was compiled as a practical guide for learners around the year 1600 by the eminent Chinese Buddhist teacher named Zhuhong.

With the discerning eye of an enlightened adept, Zhuhong assembled lessons on how to use koans that had been offered by Zen masters over many generations. Consequently this book does not represent a narrow sectarian perspective on the question of koan study, but a compendium of enlightened advice from a wide range of classic Zen teachers.

Zhuhong was a remarkable man. He lived during the last great florescence of Chinese Buddhism, in the latter part of the sixteenth century and the early part of the seventeenth century, and participated fully in the characteristic work of the Buddhist teachers of that age–reassembling the Buddhist legacy, cutting away errors and misconceptions, and disseminating the living teaching to a wide popular audience.

In his own time Zhuhong was a famous Pure Land teacher, and directed a teaching center at Yunqi Temple that was a vibrant source of Buddhist teachings to all classes of laypeople. Zhuhong was known primarily as a Pure Land adept, but he was well versed in the total heritage of Chinese Buddhism, from the scriptures and philosophical treatises, to Pure Land Buddhism and Zen. He composed guides to practice, assembled biographical information on Buddhist teachers of note, and compiled anthologies of the works of the great teachers of the past. He left a rich collection of theoretical writings on the relationship of Pure Land and Zen, and wrote often on the criteria for distinguishing genuine from false approaches to the Dharma. As a true Buddhist adept, Zhuhong recognized the value of all genuine Buddhist teachings as different means to the same end–to enable people to discover their innate potential for enlightened perception.

When reading the classic lessons on koan study assembled by Zhuhong, it is important to bear in mind that the Zen people undertook koan study in the context of a comprehensive effort to refine their behavior and mentality. Studying Zen meant a basic shift of motivations, away from the worldly, toward the world-transcending, away from ambition for personal gain, toward ideals of selfless service.

By cutting entanglements, reducing desires to a minimum, and detaching from (but not suppressing) emotions and thoughts, Zen people worked to free up the mental energy that otherwise would have been expended in the quest for worldly goals of sensory pleasure and ego gratification. It was this freed energy that was applied to koan study, and other forms of Buddhist cultivation.

To work with koans, the learner must have assimilated the basic Buddhist perspective on the fleeting nature of worldly satisfactions and the ultimate futility of craving and anger. The learner must be ready to act on the proposition that there can be more to life than the continual attempt to acquire love, honor, possessions, social standing. The learner must accept as a working hypothesis the unsettling claim that there are other ways to use mind, outside the search for animal satisfactions and culturally defined goals. The learner must be willing to venture beyond the realm of the ceaseless inner dialogue that maintains the false self by pretending that everything is already known and well-defined. These are some of the basic lessons drawn from the Buddhist teaching that must be learned as the prerequisites for koan study.

People today are ceaselessly bombarded with artful propaganda and titillating spectacles and all sorts of useless information supposed to fire their imaginations. "Attention deficit disorder" is a syndrome that increasingly afflicts all modern people.

Zen itself dates from the era before social-control-by-distraction had been raised to its present level as a major industry. But in essence the obstacles that confront modern people are only an intensified version of what always hindered people trying to learn Zen: ordinarily, all our life-energy is taken up with our mundane attachments, our craving for attention, our day-to-day plans, our hopes and fears and ambitions, and our ceaseless work of self-definition.

Once a person becomes aware of the existence Buddhist alternative, and arrives at the decision to make time to attempt to put it into practice, he or she quickly comes up against the formidable inertia of mental and behavioral routines, what the Buddhists call habit-energy. People who have tried meditation in any form quickly encounter the prodigious capacity of their minds to scatter into all sorts of random thoughts and images, or to sink down into oblivion, drifting off into sleep and dreams. Meditation with koans must also cope with problems of oblivion and scattering, and this is a topic addressed repeatedly in the lessons translated below.

In modern Western life, among ordinary, widely pursued activities, one area that offers instructive parallels to Zen practice is physical fitness training and athletics.

Certainly no one who decides to take up running after living a sedentary life expects to be able to run ten miles the first day. The only feasible approach is to start at a modest level and persist. In time, through persistent practice, one's capacity gradually builds up, and distances that were impossible at first eventually become a matter of course.

The situation with meditation work is somewhat analogous. No one who has been living the average modern life of ceaseless calculation and worry, spiced with distractions and contrived stimulation, can expect to achieve a steady and sustained focusing of attention right from the start. Anxiety, emotional turmoil, random thoughts, feelings of boredom, cravings for stimulation and distraction–these are powerful habits of mind that cannot be transformed overnight into detachment and tranquility. The capacity to focus attention on an abstract object like a koan that yields none of the usual emotional and intellectual gratifications can only be built up gradually. But in due time, with persistent effort, the person who couldn't jog a hundred yards at first can learn to run marathons.

In sports, the mark of true proficiency is when the athlete has so thoroughly internalized the proper techniques and perceptions needed in the sport that he or she puts them into practice automatically in the moment without having to think about them. The same could be said of meditation and the other central practices of Buddhism, like generosity, discipline, patience, proper application of energy, and the wisdom to see things as they are rather than as one might wish them to be. True proficiency arrives when the practitioner's mind has been restructured to the point that the Buddhist virtues are embodied spontaneously moment to moment without the need to make a deliberate effort.

The collection of Zen lessons translated below was meant for practical use. It is a reference guide for working with koans. Its instructions and examples can instruct us, inspire us, and spur us on. We can best repay Zhuhong's great compassion in composing *Impetus to Advance in the Zen Gate* by using this book as it was intended.

Impetus to Advance in the Zen Gate

Zhuhong's Preface

How could Zen be thought to have a gate? The Path [itself] has no inside or outside, no going out or going in. But when it comes to people carrying out the Path, some are deluded and some are enlightened.

Therefore, the people of knowledge, acting as the gate-keepers, have no choice but to open and close the Zen gate in a timely fashion. They are careful to keep it locked [most of the time], and rigorously check out [those who would enter]. To those whose words diverge [from the truth], those who indulge their selfishness and overstep the proper measure, the gate-keepers give no room to peddle their dishonesty. For a long time already they have barred the door to such people so they cannot easily get through.

When I first left home [and became a monk] I obtained a booklet from the booksellers called "Outline of the Buddhas and Patriarchs of the Zen School." In this book were recorded accounts given by many of the venerable adepts of old: they gave accounts of their studies, of their initial difficulties in entering [the Path], of their experiences and travail on [the Path] in doing the work, and of their final opening through into spiritual awakening. I felt great love and admiration and vowed to learn [what they had learned].

Afterwards I never again saw this book anywhere else. So I continued to read through all the recorded sayings and miscellaneous biographies in the "Five

Lamps." No matter whether they were monks or laymen, all those who engaged in real study and genuinely awakened are included in this book. I have culled out the most essential parts to form a collection, which I call "Impetus to Advance in the Zen Gate".

This book can be set on a desk when you are staying somewhere, or carried along in your bag when you travel. Once you read it, your mind and will will be stimulated and your spirit will blaze up. You will be impelled to drive yourself on to catch up with those who have gone forward [through the Zen gate] before you.

Some may say: "This collection was put together for those who have not yet passed through the gate. Those who have already passed through the gate are long gone: how can they use it?" [To them I respond:] Even though it is so, beyond this gate there is another gate. By pretending to crow like a rooster, you may temporarily escape from the tiger's mouth. But those who are satisfied with petty attainments are people with added arrogance. They have not yet come to the end of the rivers and mountains [they still have to cross].

The warning stick is in your hand: run fast and gallop on forever until you break through the ultimate mysterious barrier. Then it will not be too late to slow down and have the feast at the end of your studies.

[Dated and signed:]
First day of spring, 28th year of the Wan Li Era [1600 A.D.]
Zhuhong of Yunqi Temple

I. Essential Excerpts from the Teaching Words of the Ancestral Teachers of Zen

[Zhuhong wrote:]

Of the Dharma words of the ancestral teachers, here I do not include transcendent mystical discussions: I only select crucial points on how to do meditation work. I have limited this to the most important, most concise statements, to facilitate constant reading, and stimulate body and mind. I also follow this model in the second part, [when giving short descriptions] of the ancestral teacher's austerities, and in the final part, when assembling citations from the scriptures.

Instructions from Huangbo Xiyun [d. 850]

If you have been unable to penetrate through previously, I guarantee that when the last day of your life arrives, you will be frantic with confusion.

There are certain outsiders, who give a scoffing laugh whenever they see someone doing meditation work, and say, "You still have this one?" [as if to claim that advanced students should be beyond such deliberate practices.]

I would ask them: When suddenly you are facing the end of your lives, what will you use to fend off birth and death?

If you can accomplish [the work] when you have the free time, then you will be able to function when you are busy. How much effort this saves! Don't wait until you are thirsty to dig the well.

[If you neglect to do the work, then when death approaches], your limbs will not be properly arranged, the road ahead will be vague, and you will whirl about in confusion bumping into things. How painful!

All through your life you have only learned lip-service samadhi. You have talked of Zen and spoken of the Path, and cursed and scolded the buddhas and ancestral teachers. But when you get to this point, none of this will be of any use. Your only concern has been to deceive other people [into thinking you are wise]. You scarcely knew that when this day arrived, you would have [only] deceived yourself.

I urge all of you brothers [and sisters] to take advantage of the period when you are physically strong and healthy, to seek and find clear insight. This key link is very easy. It is just that you are not willing to mobilize your will to the utmost to do the work. All you care to do is say over and over how hard it is.

If you are for real, you will contemplate the public cases, the koans.

[For example:] A monk asked Zhaozhou, "Does a dog have buddha-nature or not?" Zhaozhou said, "No."

Contemplate this word "No" twenty-four hours a day. Study it from morning to night. Mobilize your energy and hold onto this word "No" continuously from mind-moment to mind-moment whether you are walking, standing, sitting, or lying down, whether you are dressing or eating or going to the toilet. After long days and years, you will achieve unity: unexpectedly, the mind-flower will suddenly bloom, and you will awaken to the devices of the buddhas and patriarchs.

After this you will no longer be fooled by the sayings of the world's enlightened teachers. Then you will be able to open a big mouth [and say things like] "Bodhidharma's coming from the west [to bring Zen to

China] was creating waves with no wind" and "When the World Honored One held up the flower [to start the Zen transmission in India], it was a defeat." When you reach this point, not only old man Yama [the judge of the dead], but even the thousand sages will have no way to cope with you.

[Perhaps] you do not believe me when I tell you such marvels do in fact exist. Why are you like this? "The only thing to fear is people with minds [that are already made up, and bound by conditioned opinions]."

Zhuhong's comment:

This [lesson given by Huangbo] is the starting point for [the practice] in later generations of contemplating koans.

Still, it is not necessary to hold rigidly to the word "No" [as the only koan to contemplate. You can investigate] "No" or [any of the following koans:]

"The myriad things return to one: what does the one return to?"

"What is Buddha?"–"Mount Sumeru."

"Where will you be after you have died and your body has been cremated?"

[Alternatively], you can investigate by reciting the buddha-name.

Whatever meditation point you hold to, make awakening your goal. The points of doubt may differ, but the awakening does not.

Instructions from Zen teacher Zhaozhou Congshen [778-897]

Just investigate the truth. Sit and contemplate it for twenty or thirty years. If [after that] you do not understand, you can come cut my head off.

For forty years I have not used my mind in a way that mixes [worldly concerns with the focus on truth]. My only mixed use of mind is at the two mealtimes.

Instructions from Zen teacher Xuansha Zongyi [c. 900]

To succeed as a bodhisattva learning transcendent wisdom, you must have great capacity and great wisdom.

If your faculties are slow and dull, you must endure strenuous austerities: [stay awake] day and night, oblivious of fatigue, as if you were mourning for your deceased mother.

If you act with this kind of urgency, and also obtain the support of other people [of wisdom], and make an all out effort to investigate reality, then you too will succeed.

Admonitions by Zen teacher Dayi of Goose Lake [745-818]

If you do not forget your physical form, and do not put to death your [conditioned] mind, then this incurable disease [of ignorance, craving, and aggression] is very grave.

You must take up the sword [of transcendent wisdom, which is so sharp it cuts] a hair blown across it, and cut through to the highest meaning of the Zen transmission.

Look straight at it, concentrate your attention, examine it again and again. What is it? If a person does not work hard at quiet sitting, when will he or she ever make the grade and awaken to the emptiness of mind?

Admonitions by Zen teacher Yanshou of Yongming [904-975]

There is no other special marvel in the gate of learning the Path: you simply must cleanse away the seeds of karmic consciousness [that have accumulated] over measureless eons of sensory experience.

You must be able to dissolve away feelings and thoughts, and cut off false entanglements, so that when you face all the worldly realms of craving and desire, your mind is [as inert] as wood or stone. Then even if you have not yet clarified the eye of the Path, you will spontaneously form a purified body.

If you meet a genuine guide, you must make every effort to get close to him [or her]. Even if you study with him [or her] without penetrating through [to reality], and your learning is not yet successful, what you hear from him [or her] will serve forever as seeds of the Path.

[Thenceforth], in lives to come, you will never fall into evil planes of existence [to become a hell-being, a hungry ghost, or an animal], and birth after birth you will not lose the human form. As soon as you come forth, when you hear one thing, you will understand a thousand.

Lesson given at a small gathering by Zen master Sixin Wuxin of Yellow Dragon Temple [1043-1114]

Eminent monks, it is hard to attain human form, and hard to get to hear the Buddha Dharma. If you do

not deliver this body in this lifetime, then in what lifetime will you deliver this body?

Do all of you people want to study Zen? You must
abandon something. Abandon what?   Abandon the
[physical body composed of] the four elements [fire,
water, earth, and air] and the five clusters [form, sensation, perception, motivational synthesis, consciousness].
Abandon all the karmic consciousness from countless
ages past.

Investigate what's right under your own feet. Contemplate it, get to the bottom of it. What is the truth
of it?

Keep investigating and investigating. Suddenly the
mind-flower will send forth light, shining through all the
worlds in the ten directions. Then it can be said that
"When [decisive insight] is attained from mind, it re-
sponds readily at hand."

After that you will be able to transform the earth
into gold, and churn the rivers into clarified butter. How
could you not be content and happy for life?

Do not just occupy yourself with seeking Zen and
the Path by reading words in books. The Zen Path is not
in books. Even if you read the whole Buddhist canon
and the works of all the philosophers, these are all just
idle words: when you are facing death, you will not be
able to use them at all.

Zhuhong's comment:

It would be wrong to see comments [by Zen
teachers such as those in the last paragraph] and then
denigrate the teachings of the sutras. Words like these
are meant as a warning to those who get attached to
written texts and do not cultivate the practice [of what

they teach]. They are not meant as a justification for not reading.

Lesson from Zen teacher Wuzu Fayan [d. 1104] when seeing off disciples about to embark on their travels on foot

You should take the words "birth and death" and paste them on your foreheads, and seek a clear insight into them.

If you just follow the crowd and form groups and pass your days in idle chatter, later on Old Yama [the judge of the dead] will demand an accounting from you for the money you spent on food. Don't say I didn't warn you.

In doing meditation work, you must persist in constant inquiry and always keep your attention focussed [on the main issue]: Where is power gained? Where is power not gained? Where is power lost? Where is power not lost?

There is a certain type who doze off as soon as they get on the meditation cushion. When they wake up, they are full of chaotic thoughts. As soon as they get off the meditation cushion, they are gabbing about this and that. Those who work on the Path like this will never master it even if they wait until [the Future Buddha] Maitreya is born [hundreds of thousand of years from now].

What is necessary is to boldly apply your spirit: keep your attention on a koan and study it day and night. Keep engaged with it–don't sit in the bag of unconcern. Don't sit as if dead on the meditation cushion.

With miscellaneous thoughts, the more you struggle against them, the more they come. Just very lightly abandon them. Get up and walk around a bit, then return to the meditation cushion. [Sit down] with both eyes open, close both hands into fists, and keep your spine erect: then put your attention back on the koan as you were doing before. Then you will feel pure and cool. [Putting a koan in contact with your roiling mind] is like putting a ladleful of cold water into a pot of boiling water.

If you do the work like this, the time is sure to come when you arrive home.

Open Talk by Zen Master Zhen of Yi-an at Buddha's Footprint Temple [14th century]

When belief is a hundred percent, doubt is a hundred percent. When doubt is a hundred percent, awakening is a hundred percent.

You should take all that you have seen and heard throughout your life, all your evil knowledge and understanding, all the special words and wondrous phrases like 'Zen Path' and 'Buddha Dharma', and all your attitudes of pride and arrogance, and totally pour them out.

Go to a koan you have not clearly comprehended, and plant your feet there. [Sit] with your spine erect day and night, until you do not distinguish east and west and north and south, and you are like a dead person who is still breathing.

When your mind begins to follow objects and undergo transformation, as soon as you make contact with objects, turn back [to the koan] and realize [your error]. [By doing this] your inner thoughts and concerns will naturally be forgotten, and the road of conceptual consciousness will be cut off.

Suddenly you will smash through your skull [and find that] actually, [enlightenment] is not attained from anyone else.

When that time comes, how could you not rejoice and be happy for the rest of your life?

Answers by Zen teacher Dahui Zonggao of Jingshan [1089-1163]

These days there are some [self-styled teachers] whose own eyes are not illuminated, who just teach people to stop and rest like dead jackals.

Other [false teachers] tell people to follow along with circumstances keeping [their minds] under control, to forget feelings and be silently aware. Others teach people not to be concerned with this matter [of enlightenment].

All these defective [methods of study] make you use your effort wrongly and in vain, and do not lead to complete comprehension.

Just keep your mind in one place, and attainment is certain. When the [right] juncture of time and circumstances arrives, you will naturally bump right into it, and awaken with a start.

Take your own consciousness, which is entangled with worldly afflictions, and move it back onto transcendent wisdom.

[If you do this consistently, then] even if you do not penetrate all the way through in this lifetime, you definitely will not be dragged off by evil karma at the end of your life. When you emerge again in a future birth, you are sure to be in the midst of transcendent wisdom, and receive the use of it ready-made. This is something definite beyond a doubt.

Just keep your attention focussed [on the koan] all the time. When false thoughts arise, do not try to use mind to stop them. Just contemplate the koan. Keep your attention focussed on it when you are walking and keep your attention focussed on it when you are sitting. Keep on and on focussing your attention on it.

When there is no flavor, no interest, this is a good time: do not abandon it. Suddenly the mind-flower comes to light, and shines on all the worlds in the ten directions. Then you will be able to manifest the Land of the Jewel King inside a single pore, and turn the Great Dharma Wheel while seated within an atom of dust.

Zhuhong's Comment:

Dahui himself said: "With other people, concentration is first, and afterwards wisdom. With me, wisdom is first, and afterwards concentration."

In sum, [what Dahui is saying in this quote is that] if you smash through your doubt over the koan [and open through to wisdom], then the so-called stopping and resting [achieved by concentration] will happen without having to be aimed for.

An Account of Personal Experience from Zen teacher Mengshan Deyi [b. 1231]

When I was twenty years old, I knew about the existence of this affair [of enlightenment]. By the time I was thirty-two, I had called on seventeen or eighteen elders and asked them for instruction. I questioned them about doing [meditation] work, but none of them had it right.

Later on I studied with the Elder of Wanshan. He taught me to contemplate the word "No". He told me that [while contemplating "No"] I should be as attentive as a cat stalking a mouse, or a chicken incubating an egg, twenty-four hours a day, and not allow any interruptions. Before I penetrated through, I should be like a rat gnawing on a coffin: I should not shift [my attention]. If I acted like this, [he assured me], there would surely be a time when illumination developed.

So I worked hard investigating [the meditation point "No"] day and night for eighteen days. As I was drinking tea, suddenly I was able to understand [the meaning of] the World Honored One holding up the flower [to communicate his ineffable message], and Kashyapa smiling [in tacit comprehension].

I was overjoyed, and went to seek confirmation from three or four elder [Zen men I knew], but they didn't have a word to say. Someone told me to take the ocean seal samadhi and seal [everything with it]. I paid no attention to anything else, and just trusted in this advice.

Two years passed. It was the sixth month of 1264. I was in [the city of] Chungking in Sichuan [in Western China] ill with dysentery. Many many times through the days and nights I was in extreme danger and on the verge of death.

[I discovered to my chagrin that from all my previous religious efforts] I had gotten no power whatsoever. I could not use the ocean seal samadhi, or any of what I had previously understood. I had a mouth but could not speak, I had a body but could not move. All there was for me to do was die.

40   *Meditating with Koans*

Scenes brought on by karmic entanglements all
began to appear before me at that moment. I was terri-
fied, panic stricken. All kinds of suffering were closing
in on me.

I forced myself to act the master, and gave instructions for posthumous arrangements. I placed the meditation cushion up high, and set out a brazier full of incense. Then I very slowly arose and went to sit in meditation. Silently I prayed to the Buddha, Dharma, and
Sangha, and to the nagas and devas. I repented all my
previous bad deeds.

[I took the following vow]: If my life is about to
end, may I take advantage of the power of transcendent
wisdom, and be reborn with correct mindfulness, so that
I leave home [to become a monk] early on [in my next
life]. If I am cured of this sickness, then I promise to
abandon lay life and become a monk, so that I may soon
attain enlightenment, and work on a broad scale for the
salvation of younger students.

After making this vow, I put my attention on the
word "No", turned the light around, and observed
myself.

Before very long, I felt my guts churning, but I paid
no attention to anything else [but the word "No"]. I went
on for a long time without moving my eyelids. More
time passed and I no longer saw my body there: just the
koan, uninterrupted.

When night came I finally got up: my sickness had
abated halfway. I resumed sitting [in meditation], and
sat until the middle of the night. The sickness left me
completely, and my body and mind felt at ease.

In the eighth month [of that year] I went to [the city
of] Jiangling and was ordained as a monk there. For a
year I travelled on foot, cooking my meals by the road-

side. I realized that meditation work must be done with all one's energy, and its continuity should not be broken.

When I went to Yellow Dragon Temple, I went back to the meditation hall [and proceeded to my meditation work]. The first time the demon of sleep came, without leaving the meditation seat I aroused my spirit and without great effort fought it back. The second time the demon of sleep also retreated like this. The third time the demon of sleep was heavy, and I got down on the floor to do prostrations to dispel it, then went back to the meditation cushion. When I was settled in the proper posture, I used this time to vanquish the demon of sleep.

At first [when I needed to take a break from sitting meditation], I would use a pillow and sleep for a short period of time. Later [I napped] with my arm [as a pillow]. Later I would not let my body lie down. After two or three days [of sitting meditation without lying down], I would feel tired day and night, and I seemed to be floating along over the ground.

Suddenly it was as if the black clouds before my eyes cleared away. My body felt as if it had been newly washed, and a pure happiness poured forth from it. In my mind the mass of doubt was more and more intense, and it appeared before me continuously with no effort on my part. No sound or form, no desires, no bad influences could enter [my mind]: it was as pure as a silver bowl filled with snow, as crisp as the autumn air.

But then I thought to myself, though my meditation work is good, I have no one who can sort it out for me. So I took up my mat and went to Zhejiang [province on the central coast of China]. On the way I encountered hardships, and my meditation work regressed.

I came to Master Guchan's place at Tiancheng Temple and went back to the meditation hall. I swore to myself that I would not move again until I attained illumination.

For a month and more I did meditation work as I had before. At that time, my whole body was covered with ulcers, but I paid no attention. I had abandoned my life to pursue the work, and naturally I found power. Again I was doing meditation work in the midst of sickness.

Once I went out to attend a vegetarian feast, holding my attention on the koan as I walked along, and unknowingly walked past the house where the feast was being held. So I was also doing meditation work while moving.

When I reached this point, it seemed that [I had reached the state described in the Zen saying]: "The moonlight shining through the water can meet the rapids without being scattered and wash through the chaotic waves without being lost." I was leaping with life.

On the sixth day of the third month, as I was sitting with my attention correctly focussed on the word "No", the head monk entered the hall to burn incense. He struck the incense bowl and it made a sound: suddenly at the sound of the blow, I knew that I had found myself, and that I had captured Zhaozhou [the Zen teacher who originally posed the koan "No"].

Then I spoke a verse:

> Unexpectedly the road ends
> I kick it over: the waves are water
> Old Zhaozhou goes beyond the crowd
> His face is just like this

That autumn in [the city of] Lin'an I met several great Zen elders: Qin of Xueyan, Ning of Tuigeng, Yan of Shifan, and Du of Xuzhou. Du of Xuzhou urged me to go to visit Zen master Wanshan.

[When I got there] Wanshan [used a classical Zen verse] to question me: "'Glorious light silently shining, pervading countless worlds': aren't these the words of Zhang Zhuo?" As I opened my mouth [to speak], Wanshan gave a shout and left. From then on, whether I was walking, sitting, eating, or drinking, I had no thoughts at all.

Six months passed. In the spring of the following year, as I was returning from a trip to the city, I was climbing up some stone stairs, when suddenly the obstruction of doubt in my breast melted away forever. I was walking along the road unaware of having a body.

When I met with Wanshan, he asked me the same question as before. I immediately overturned the meditation bench. I clearly understood every one of the koans I had previously found extremely obscure.

Good people, studying Zen requires careful, thorough work. If I had not become sick at Chungking, I probably would have passed my life in vain.

The crucial thing is to meet a person with correct knowledge. This is why the ancients studied and asked for instruction from morning to night, to get mind and body decisively sorted out. They worked hard and worked urgently to investigate and illuminate this affair [of enlightenment].

Instructions from Layman Tian of Su-an [c. 1280]

In recent years, those who are sincere about studying Zen have been few. As soon as people come to grips with a koan, they are tied up by the two demons of oblivion and scattering. They do not know that oblivion and scattering are to be opposed with the sentiment of doubt. If belief is strong, then the sentiment of doubt is sure to be strong. If the sentiment of doubt is strong, then oblivion and scattering will automatically be nullified.

Open talk by Zen teacher Cang of Baiyun Wuliang Temple
[who was the spiritual "grandson" of Tian of Su-an]

Twenty-four hours a day, walk along with the koan, stand along with the koan, sit along with the koan, and lie down along with the koan.

Let your mind be like a thicket of brambles. Do not let it be swallowed up by such things as [notions] of self and others, ignorance, desires for food, sex, sleep, wealth, and fame, or craving, aggression, and folly.

Whether walking, standing, sitting, or lying down, your whole body should be a mass of doubt. Keep on doubting and doubting. All day long be insensitive to sound and form. I guarantee the burst of power will come.

Answer to a Zen man's letter by Zen teacher Qin of Siming Yonggang

To do meditation work, you must arouse great doubt. Your work will not be completed in only a month or half a month. If true doubt appears, it cannot be shaken. Naturally you will not fear becoming confused. Just be bold and determined and press onward. Go all day long like an idiot. At such a time there is no fear that "the turtle will get out of the bottle" [that your focussed attention will stray from the koan].

Open talk by Zen teacher Xueyan Zuqin   [d. 1287]

Time does not wait for people: a blink of the eye and it's already a future birth.

Better take advantage of [the time when] your body is strong and healthy to penetrate all the way through and find clear understanding.

Will you be so lucky [in your future lives] as to attain again this fair setting, this world of spirit dragons, this Dharma-cave of enlightened teachers, this clear, clean monks' hall, this wholesome food, the security of this warm hearth?

If you do not penetrate through and find clear understanding while you are here, you have injured yourself, you have forsaken yourself, you have consented to sink yourself to the level of the lowest, stupidest fools.

If you are really confused and totally without knowledge, why don't you go and ask many questions of those who have gone before you who do know? Whenever you meet them, try to learn from them. When you see old fellows up on the teacher's seat talking of this and that, why don't you listen carefully, and consider again and again what truth it ultimately is [that they're expressing]?

I left home when I was five, and became an attendant to an eminent monk. Seeing him converse with guests, I became aware of the existence of this matter [of enlightenment]. I immediately had full faith in it, and so I began to learn how to do sitting meditation.

When I was sixteen, I became a monk. At eighteen, I went travelling on foot. I joined Master Yuan's congregation at Shuanglin Temple. From morning to night I never left the yard. Even when I went to the assembly hall, I went to the very back. I kept my hands in my sleeves folded to my chest, and never glanced left or right. I saw no more than three feet in front of me.

At first I contemplated the word "No". When a thought suddenly arose, I would look back on it, and the thought would immediately freeze. I became clear all the way through, unmoving and unwavering. A whole day would pass like a snap of the fingers: I did not hear the sounds of the bell and drum [marking the temple routine] at all.

When I was nineteen, I settled at Lingyuan Temple. There I met a secretary who had come from [the city of] Chuzhou. He said to me, "Qin, your meditation work is stagnant, and does not accomplish anything. You have arbitrarily separated the two forms–movement and stillness. To study Zen, one must arouse the sentiment of doubt. From small doubt, there is small awakening; from great doubt, great awakening."

After the secretary from Chuzhou had criticized me so aptly, I changed my koan, and contemplated the saying "What is Buddha?"–"A dry piece of shit."

I went on consistently doubting and doubting and contemplating [this koan] up and down and back and forth. When I was assailed by oblivion and scattering, in a short time I would cleanse them away. But I could not succeed.

I moved to Pure Compassion Temple and formed a group with seven of the brethren to do sitting meditation. We pledged ourselves not to let our sides touch our mats [to sit in meditation through the night without lying down].

Besides us, there was an advanced monk named Xiu, who sat everyday on his meditation cushion like an iron rod. When he walked around, he opened his eyes and hung his arms down, but he was still like an iron rod. I wanted to approach him and talk to him, but it was impossible.

After two years without lying down, I ended up in a hazy state of mind, exhausted. Then as soon as I let myself go [and lay down], I let go completely. After two months, I recovered to the way I was before: after getting this release, my spirit was totally restored.

Actually, if you want to investigate and understand this matter, going without sleep will not do. What is required is to sleep soundly till the middle of the night, then suddenly awaken: only then will the spirit be there.

One day I met Xiu on the veranda, and finally was able to approach him. I asked, "Last year I wanted to talk with you, but you just avoided me: why?"

Xiu said, "A person who is truly working on the Path does not have time to cut his nails, much less to talk with you."

I said, "Even now, I have not yet banished oblivion and scattering."

Xiu said, "Since you are not bold enough, you must go sit on the meditation cushion, hold your spine erect, and gather your whole body together into a koan. What more oblivion and scattering will there be to look for then?"

I practiced meditation work as Xiu had told me. Before I knew it, body and mind were both forgotten, and I remained completely pure for three days and nights without closing my eyes.

It was afternoon on the third day and I was walking by the temple gate in the same state of mind as when I had been sitting. I again bumped into Xiu.

He asked me, "What are you doing here?"

I said, "Working on the Path."

Xiu said, "What are you calling 'the Path'?"

I could not answer, and felt even more confused and depressed. I was about to return to the hall to sit in meditation, when I met the head monk. He told me, "Open your eyes wide and observe what truth it is." Having had this phrase brought to my attention, I just wanted to go back to the meditation hall.

As soon as I sat on the meditation cushion, what was before my eyes emptied out and opened up, like the ground falling away.

At the time I could not tell anyone what it was like, because it was not something that could be described with worldly attributes. So I left the meditation seat and went looking for Xiu.

As soon as Xiu saw me he said, "How happy you are! How happy I am for you!" He took me by the hand and we walked around the willowy embankment in front of the temple gate.

As I looked up and down between the sky and the earth, [I realized that] the whole dense array of myriad images, all that my eyes saw and my ears heard, all the things that I had previously felt disgusted with and tried to abandon as the afflictions of ignorance—all of this was actually flowing forth from my own wondrous, illuminated true nature.

For more than half a month no signs of motion were born. It is too bad that [at that point] I did not meet an experienced adept with great abilities and great discernment. I should not have settled down here [in this motionlessness]. It is said that if you do not slough off the stage of se*eing*, it blocks true perception.

Whenever I went to sleep, [my realization] broke in two. Koans that had an obvious meaning I could understand rationally, but those that were like a silver mountain or an iron wall, I did not understand.

Though I was in the assembly of my late master Wuzhun for many years, and entered his room and ascended the seat [to preach], not a word [of what he said] got through to what was on my mind. The scriptures and the recorded sayings [of the earlier Zen masters] likewise had nothing to say that could release me from this sickness.

I went on like this, blocked within my breast, for ten years.

One day I was walking in the buddha-shrine at Tianmu Temple, when I glanced up and saw an ancient pine tree. As my eyes made contact with it, insight came forth, and the realm that I had previously attained, the thing that had obstructed me, tumbled down and dispersed. It was like going from a dark room out into the bright sunlight.

After this I had no doubts about birth or death, about buddhas or patriarchs. I finally saw [the meaning of the saying by] the old man of Jingshan: "Right where you stand, you deserve thirty blows."

Instructions from Zen teacher Gaofeng Yuanmiao [1238-1295]
[a disciple of Xueyan Zuqin]

This matter [of developing enlightened perception] only requires that the person concerned truly has a serious attitude.

As soon as you have a serious attitude, then true doubt arises. Keep on doubting and doubting: start doubting what you don't doubt. From morning to evening, from head to tail, fuse [yourself and your doubt] into one whole. Let it become unshakeable and impossible to dispel, shining with spiritual awareness, constantly appearing before you. This is the time when you gain power.

In addition, you must focus your correct mindfulness, and be careful not to have anything else on your mind.

Get to the point that you walk without knowing you're walking, and sit without knowing you're sitting, and don't notice cold or heat or hunger of thirst.

When this realm appears before you, this is the scene where you arrive home. Here you can reach it and touch it.

All you can do is wait for the right moment. You must not see this kind of talk and become zealous to seek it. Nor should you take your mind and wait for it. Nor should you indulge [your mind] or abandon it. Just strengthen and consolidate correct mindfulness, and take enlightenment as the standard.

Right now there is an army of eighty-four thousand demons of delusion standing by at the doors of your six senses. All sorts of unusual and strange things, both good and evil, manifest themselves following your mind. If even for a moment you give rise to the slightest attitude of attachment, you will immediately fall into their trap: you will be dominated by them and be at their command. Then your mouth will speak the words of delusion and your body will perform the actions of delusion. Because of this, the correct basis for transcendent wisdom will be forever cut off and the seeds of enlightenment will never again sprout.

Just do not give rise to [deluded attached states of] mind. Be like a ghost guarding a corpse. Keep on guarding it and guarding it. The mass of doubt will heat up and finally explode: I guarantee it will startle the heavens and shake the earth.

I was fifteen when I left home. At twenty I became a monk and entered Pure Compassion Temple. I set myself a firm three-year limit to learn Zen.

At first I studied with the Master of Broken Bridge, who directed me to come to grips [with the koan] "Where do we come from when we're born and where do we go when we die?" [As I came to grips with this koan] my thinking divided this into two routes, and my mind did not return to their unity.

Later I met Master Xueyan Zuqin, who told me to contemplate the word "No". He also directed me to come up [to his private quarters and consult him] every day, like a man on a journey who wants to check his progress every day. Thus I saw that there was a systematic order in what he said.

Later on [one day when I came to his room], he did not ask about my practice, but as soon as I came in the door, he asked me, "Who is hauling this dead body in here for you?" Then, before he finished asking, he drove me out with blows.

Subsequently I went back to the monks' hall at Jingshan. In a dream I suddenly recalled [the koan] "The myriad things return to one: what does the one return to?" At this, the feeling of doubt suddenly came forth, so that I no longer kept track of where I was.

On the sixth day [after this], I went along with a group of monks into a room to recite scriptures. I raised my head and suddenly saw a portrait of Master Wuzu Fayan. The portrait bore an inscription, of which the last two lines read:

One hundred years, thirty-six thousand mornings
Going back and forth, all along it was this guy.

Suddenly I broke through the saying from the day
before about hauling the dead body. My soul flew up
and my guts dropped out: after annihilation, came re-
birth. It was like putting down a hundred pound load.

When this happened, I was exactly twenty-four
years old: I had fulfilled the three year limit [I had set for
myself to learn Zen].

After this, I was questioned by [Master Zuqin]. He
asked, "Can you act the master in the midst of your busy
everyday life?" I answered that I could. He also asked,
"Can you act the master in your dreams?" I answered
that I could. He asked, "When you are in a dreamless
sleep, where is the master?" There was nothing I could
say in reply to this, no reasoning I could put forward.

Master Zuqin instructed me [as follows]: "From now
on, I do not want you to study the Buddha Dharma or
investigate [the sayings of] ancient and modern [Zen
teachers]. Just eat when hungry and sleep when tired.
As soon as you awaken from sleep, mobilize your spirit
[and ponder this question:] 'Ultimately where does the
master of this wakefulness of mine put his body and
his life?'"

I swore to stake my whole life [on this question]: I
would act oblivious of everything else, determined to
see clearly into this issue.

Almost five years passed. One morning I awoke, in
doubt over this issue. The companion in the Path with
whom I was sharing lodgings unexpectedly pushed his
pillow and it fell to the ground making a sound.

Suddenly I smashed my mass of doubt. I was like
leaping out of a net. I completely understood all the
inexplicable koans of the buddhas and patriarchs and all

the ancient and modern "differentiating stories" [which Zen adepts use to sort out the experiential states of their students].

From then on, the land was secure and the state firmly established: all under heaven enjoyed Great Peace. With unified mindfulness free from contrived activity I cut off everything in the ten directions.

Zhuhong's comment:

The foregoing passage instructing the assembly on how to do meditation work is very concise and important. Students should "inscribe it on their belts" [refer to it constantly].

What it says in the account about "Eating when hungry and sleeping when tired" is something for *after* illumination [not before]. Do not misunderstand this.

Open talk by Zen teacher Qiong of Iron Mountain [later 13th century]

I was thirteen years old when I became aware of the existence of the Buddha Dharma. At eighteen I left home, and at twenty-two I became a monk.

First I went to Shishuang Temple. I remember that Hermit Xiang taught us always to focus our attention on the end of our noses, and thus we would attain purity.

Later a monk came from Xueyan. He wrote out a copy of his master's "Guidelines for Sitting Meditation" for us to read. We had been doing meditation work, but we had never proceeded as Xueyan directed in this book.

So I went to Xueyan and meditated according to his teaching. I put my attention on the word "No". On the fourth night, my whole body was dripping with sweat. I was totally purified and refreshed. Right after that I went back to the hall. I did not speak with anyone, but concentrated on sitting in meditation.

Later I met Master Gaofeng Yuanmiao. He taught me [as follows]:

"[Meditate continuously] twenty-four hours a day and do not let there be any interruptions. Arise long before dawn, gather up the koan, and put it before you. If you feel the least bit sleepy, get up [from the meditation seat] and walk around, still [with your attention on] the koan. With every step you take while walking, do not depart from the koan. Whether spreading out your mat, or holding out your bowl, or lifting up your spoon, or putting down your chopsticks, or following along with the congregation, never depart from the koan. Carry on like this all through the day and all through the night. All those who fuse themselves into one whole [with the koan] will surely develop illumination."

I did the meditation work according to Gaofeng's instructions, and actually became fused [with the koan].

On the twelfth day of the third month, Xueyan [Zuqin] came up to the meditation hall and said:

"Brothers, when you have been sitting on the meditation cushion for a long time and begin to get sleepy, you must get down and walk around a bit. Wash with cold water until your eyes are [fully] open [again], then get back on the meditation cushion. Hold your backbone erect, towering up like a wall miles high, and concentrate on the koan. Work like this for seven days, and you will certainly awaken. This is the work I have done for the past forty years."

I immediately proceeded to follow what Gaofeng and Xueyan had said, and I felt that [this method of] meditation work was different from my usual way.

On the second day, my eyes wanted to shut, but I could not shut them. By the third day, my body felt as if I was walking through empty space. By the fourth day, I was no longer aware of the existence of worldly affairs.

That night I stood for a little while leaning against the balustrade, obliterated, oblivious, checking out the koan. Without losing track of it, I turned around to go back to the meditation cushion, when suddenly I felt from head to toe like my skull was being split apart. It was like being hoisted from the bottom of a well miles deep up into the sky.

At this moment there was no room in me for joy. I told Xueyan about [my experience], and he said, "You're not there yet. Go work at it some more." I sought some words of instruction [from him].

At the end [of our meeting] he told me, "To perpetuate the transcendent affair of the buddhas and patriarchs and make it flourish, you are still lacking a hammerblow to the back of the head. In your mind say [to yourself], 'How can I still be lacking a hammerblow?'"

I did not believe these words, and again I seemed to have doubt. I could not resolve it. Every day I would pile up [my doubt] and sit in meditation. Almost half a year had gone by when one day I had a headache, so I brewed up some medicine [and drank it]. As I noticed my red nose, I recalled being asked by Wu, the monk in charge of guests, about the story of Prince Nata carving out his bones to give back to his father and slicing off his flesh to give back to his mother. I had been unable to reply. Suddenly I smashed this mass of doubt [about what Xueyan intended when he told me I was not there yet].

Later I went to [Zen teacher] Mengshan. Mengshan asked me, "In studying Zen, what is the point you have to arrive at for your work to be finished?"

I did not know [the answer]. Mengshan directed me to work some more on my power of concentration, and wash away my sensory habits. Every time I went into his room to say something, he would just tell me that I was still lacking.

One day I sat from late afternoon through the night, pressing hard with the power of concentration, until I reached [an experiential realm of] abstruse rarefied subtlety.

When I came out of my concentration, I went to see Mengshan. After I had told him about this realm, he asked, "What is your original face?"

Just as I was about to say something, Mengshan closed his door [in my face]. From then on, every day in my meditation work I had wondrous experiences.

Because I had left Xueyan too early, I had not done [enough] careful, thorough meditation work. I was lucky enough to meet a genuine craftsman of the Zen school [like Mengshan], and so I managed to reach this level. Actually, if one can do the work rigorously, then there will be awakenings time after time, and the splitting off and falling away [of delusions] with every step.

One day I happed to see written on a wall the Third Patriarch's *Inscription of the Mind of Faith* which says: "Return to the root and find the true meaning. Follow the awareness and lose the basic principle." [When I saw this passage] I stripped off another layer.

Mengshan said [to me at this point], "This affair is like peeling layers off a pearl. The more layers you peel off, the brighter it shines; the more illumination, the more purity. Peel them off: it's better than several lifetimes of meditation work. But if you say something, I'll still just tell you that you're lacking."

One day in the midst of my concentration I suddenly touched on the word *lacking*. My body and mind emptied out to the core. It was like a pile of snow abruptly melting away. I could not suppress a smile.

I jumped up off the meditation seat and grabbed hold of Mengshan and said, "What am I lacking?" Mengshan gave me three slaps, and I bowed down to him three times.

Mengshan said, "How many years you have been at this! Today you have finally finished."

If the koan is temporarily absent, you are like a dead man. When all sorts of scenes press in on you, take the koan and fend them off. Be checking out the koan at all times, while you are moving and while you are still, whether you gain power or whether you don't. Nor should you forget the koan in the midst of concentration: if you forget it, then it becomes misguided concentration.

Do not hold to mind and await enlightenment. Do not grasp interpretive understanding based on words. Do not think you are finished with things when you get a bit of awakening. Just go on like an ignoramus. Fuse the Buddha Dharma and worldly phenomena into one. [After enlightenment] your conduct and actions will be ordinary: all that has been changed is the former locus of your activities.

An ancient said, "The Great Path has never been in the province of words. If you attempt to speak of the mystic wonder, you are as far apart from it as the heavens from the abyss. You must forget both subject and object: only then can you eat when hungry and sleep when tired."

Instructions from Zen Master Liaoyi of Broken Cliff [1263-1334]

If you want to transcend the ordinary and enter sagehood, and forever shed sensory afflictions, you must strip off your skin and change your bones [shift the basis of your experience from conditioned perceptions to reality itself]

After annihilation, you are reborn: it is like flames flaring up in the cold ashes, like a dead tree blooming again. How could this be easy to conceive of?

I was in the congregation of my late teacher [Gaofeng Yuanmiao] for many years. Even when I was severely beaten, I had no thought of leaving. Even now, whenever I come in contact with something painful, my tears flow without me being aware of it. How does this compare with you, who hang your heads and won't look when you taste some bitterness?

Instructions from Zen teacher Zhongfeng Mingben [1263-1323]

My late teacher Gaofeng Yuanmiao taught people to hold within them nothing but the koan they were studying. [He said] that they should study like this whether they were walking or sitting, and study to the point where all exertions come up short.

Then, when [students engaged in this sort of practice] were concerned that they would not succeed, suddenly they would break through: only then would they know that they had attained enlightenment, and that it had been coming for a long time.

This strategy has already been proven effective by all the buddhas and enlightened teachers since antiq-

uity. It is the state of concentration for complete liberation from birth and death. All that is important is to have
complete faith in it, and [persevere in it] for a long time
without turning back. [If you do so], then it is impossible
not to get its results.

You may go twenty or thirty years without opening
up to enlightenment. You don't have to seek any other
means: simply do not involve your mind with other entanglements, and cut off all falsity from your thoughts.
Work hard and don't give up.

Just plant your feet firmly on the koan you are
studying. Go all out: if it is born, be born along with it;
if it dies, die along with it. No matter whether it takes
three lifetimes or five lifetimes or ten lifetimes or a hundred lifetimes, be sure not to stop until you have penetrated through to enlightenment.

If you have this correct basis [in genuine aspiration
and rightly guided practice], do not worry that you will
not completely illuminate the great matter [of enlight-
enment].

To do meditation work when you are sick, it is not
necessary for you to be energetic and vigorous, and it is
not necessary for you open your eyes wide and stare.
All that is necessary is for your mind to be like wood or
stone, and you thoughts to be like dead ashes. Take the
illusory body composed of the four elements and cast it
off beyond the world.

If you follow this, then you will succeed even if
you are sick; you will succeed whether you live or die;
you will succeed if someone is watching you or if
no one is watching you; you will succeed whether you
are fragrant and fresh or stinking and rotten; you will

succeed if you are cured and regain your health and live to be a hundred and twenty; you will succeed if you die and are dragged off to the torments of hell by your past deeds.

In all these situations, do not waver. Just resolutely take the flavorless koan and put it beside your medicine burner, next to your [sickbed] pillow, and silently inquire into it: you must not abandon it.

Zhuhong's comment:

All the words of these elders [I have quoted above] just teach people to contemplate koans, to do genuine meditation work, in order to aim for true enlightenment. They are vital, reliable instructions, lucid and lively.

For a thousand years, there have been such earnest, emphatic lessons [offered by the masters of the Zen tradition]. Those who have the complete texts [from which these excerpts are drawn] should read them in their entirety.

Open talk by Zen teacher Weize of Tianru Temple on Lion Peak

[died 1354; a disciple of Zhongfeng Mingben]

If you do not know where you come from when you are born, then you think birth is a big thing.

If you do not know where you are going when you die, then you think death is a big thing.

When the last day of your life arrives, you will fall into bodily confusion: the road ahead is vague. You will receive retribution according to your deeds. The crucial matter lies in this: this is the reward of birth and death.

As for the karmic root of birth and death, it is this present moment of thought that follows sounds and pursues forms, and makes you upside-down. It was for this reason that the buddhas and ancestral teachers set in motion their great compassion. Sometimes they taught you to study Zen. Sometimes they taught you to recite the buddha-name. They enabled you to sweep away false thoughts, recognize your original face, and be a person of great liberation, untrammeled and free.

Among people today who do not obtain the spiritual effects [of the Buddhist teachings] there are three kinds of sickness.

The first is not to encounter the instructions of a genuine enlightened teacher.

The second is to be unable to take the great matter of birth and death seriously, to act with unrestrained self-indulgence, and unwittingly put yourself into the bag of unconcern.

The third is to be unable to see through and abandon the empty fame and fleeting fortune of worldly life, to be unable to cut off and get clear of false entanglements and evil habits. Then when the wind of objects blows, your body is tumbled unawares into the sea of karma to drift hither and yon.

How could those who are truly people of the Path be willing to act this way? You should have confidence in the Path of the buddhas and ancestral teachers.

How should you set to work on miscellaneous thoughts flying around in confusion? A koan is like a broom made of iron. The more you sweep, the more [wandering thoughts] there are; the more there are, the more you sweep. When you cannot sweep [any more], go all out and keep sweeping. Suddenly you will sweep through to the great void, [and find] a single

road going through the myriad distinctions and differences.

You worthy followers of Zen: if you try hard, you
are sure to finish in this lifetime. Do not let yourselves
go on [deluded], suffering further disasters for end-
less ages!

There are those who have doubts about the differences between reciting the buddha-name and studying
Zen. They do not realize that the purpose of studying
Zen is to recognize mind and see our real nature, and
that those reciting the buddha-name awaken to the
Amitabha of inherent nature and the Pure Land of mind-
only. How could there be two [different] principles here?

The scripture says: "Remember buddha, recite the
buddha-name, and in the present or the future you are
sure to see buddha."   Since [this Pure Land scripture]
speaks of seeing buddha in the present, how is it any
different from awakening to the Path by studying Zen?

Just take the words 'Amitabha Buddha' and make
them a koan. Keep your attention on this koan consistently twenty-four hours a day. When you reach the
point where not a thought is born, you will directly pass
over to the stage of buddhahood without going through
any steps or levels.

Zen teacher Zhizhe's *Pure Land Mystic Gate*
[14th century]

Recite the buddha-name once, or perhaps three
times or five times or seven times. Silently turn back and
ask, "Where does this recitation of the buddha-name

arise?" Also ask, "Who is this one reciting the buddha-name?" If you have doubts, just go right ahead and doubt. If the way you pose these questions is not on an intimate level, then your feeling of doubt will not be urgent.

Again, focus your attention on [the koan]: "Who ultimately is the one reciting the buddha-name?"

Inquire a little into the first question, and have a little doubt about it. Carefully and exhaustively investigate and inquire into "Who is the one reciting the buddha-name?"

Zhuhong's comment:

In the direct route [of combining Pure Land and Zen practice], the first question can be ignored. You will succeed anyway if you just contemplate "Who is the one reciting the buddha-name?"

Open talk by Zen teacher Wuwen Cong of Fragrant Mountain

At the beginning [of my Zen studies] I met Master Duweng. He directed me to study [the saying] "It is not mind, it is not buddha, it is not things." Later I took a vow along with six other men, including Yunfeng, Yueshan, and others, to investigate it to the end together.

Next I met Jiao Wuneng of Huaixi. He directed me to keep my attention on the word "No".

Then I went to Changlu and formed a group of companions so we could refine and polish [our understanding].

Finally I encountered Brother Jing of Huaishang. He asked me, "After your six or seven years [of meditation work], what level of perception do you have?"

I answered, "Every day there is not a single thing in my mind."

Jing said, "Where did this rope that you have wound around you come from?"

In my mind I seemed to know, but I did not know, so I did not dare open my mouth.

Seeing by how I acted that I had developed no insight, Jing then said, "If you do not lose it in the midst of the concentration of your meditation work, then you lose it when you are in motion." As he spoke to me, I felt startled. Then I asked, "Ultimately, to illuminate this great matter, what must I do?"

Jing said, "Haven't you heard old man Chuan's saying? 'If you want to know the true meaning, see the Northern Dipper while facing south.'" After he said this, he left.

[From the impact of] being questioned by Jing, I got so that I was walking without knowing I was walking, and sitting without knowing I was sitting. For seven days or so, I did not meditate on the word "No". Instead, I contemplated [the koan] "If you want to know the true meaning, see the Northern Dipper while facing south".

Suddenly [without knowing how I'd gotten there] I was in the sweeper's shed sitting on a log with a group of people. My feeling of doubt had not dissipated. It was time to eat when suddenly my mind felt empty and bright and light and pure. My views, feelings, and thoughts shattered. It was as if I had peeled off my skin. I saw nothing of the people and things in front of my eyes: it was like empty space.

After a half hour I came out of it, and my whole body was dripping with sweat. Then I awakened to "seeing the Northern Dipper while facing south".

Later I met Brother Jing and I was able to speak [to him about my state] and make up verses [about it] without any hindrance at all. I still had the one road of transcendence, but I was not yet totally free.

Later I went to Fragrant Cliff Mountain and passed the summer there. My hands couldn't keep still when I was bitten by mosquitos. I thought of the ancients who had forgotten their bodies for the sake of the Dharma. "Why should I be afraid of mosquitos?" [I asked myself]. So I wholeheartedly relinquished [all my vexation and concern].

I clenched my teeth, closed my hands into fists, put my undivided attention on the word "No." I persevered and kept at it.

Without my being aware of it, my body and mind returned to stillness. It was like the four walls of a house falling down. My body was like empty space, and there was not a single thing to occupy my feelings. I began sitting around nine in the morning and came out of my concentration around three in the afternoon.

I realized that the Buddha Dharma does not lead people astray: it's just that their work is not complete.

Though my perception was clear, I still had slight traces of hidden false thoughts that were not yet exhausted. I went to Guangzhou Mountain and practiced concentration there for six years. I then lived for six years at Lu-an Mountain, and then three more years at Guangzhou Mountain: only then did I emerge into complete liberation.

Zhuhong's comment:

Only when the people of olden times had worked this hard, and this long, did they attain accord [with reality].

Today's people use their intelligence and senti-mental assessments and get understanding in a minute, yet they want to credit themselves with sudden enlight-enment. This is surely a mistake!

Instructions from Master Dufeng

Where should people who study the Path set to work? They should put their attention on a koan: this is where to set to work.

Instructions from Master Panruo [Juexue Shicheng, 1270-1342]

Brothers [and sisters], if you meditate for four or five years without an entry [into enlightenment], and you abandon the koan you have been using all that time, don't you know that this is like abandoning a journey when you are halfway there? What a pity that so much previous mental effort [will have been wasted].

People who are intent [on enlightenment] observe that the congregation has firewood and ample water and that the monks' hall is warm. They vow that they will not go out the gate for three years, and resolve to gain the use [of their buddha-nature].

There are some whose mind-ground becomes clear as soon as they start meditation work. But when they see scenes and objects appear before them [in their meditation], they conceive of them as existent, or as empty, or as both existent and empty, or as neither existent nor empty. They think [that being aware of these ontological permutations means] they are people of great correct comprehension. With their facile tongues, they pass their lives sunk in error. When their physical vitality dissolves away, how will they preserve [their awareness]?

Children of Buddha, if you want to get beyond [these errors], when you study it must be genuine study, and when you awaken it must be real awakening.

Some people have complete continuity with [their attention on] the koan, without any breaks, until they become unaware of having a body. They think this is [what is referred to in the Zen expression] "person forgotten, things not yet forgotten."

Some come to this stage of forgetting their own body, and then suddenly remember it. This is like slipping off a precipice in a dream, and being so frantic to save your life that you go crazy.

When you get to this stage [where you forget your body], you must urgently keep your attention on the koan: suddenly, everything is forgotten, even the koan. This is called "person and things both forgotten". Suddenly "in the cold ashes, the kernel pops" [amidst total dispassion and detachment, delusion breaks up].

Then at last you know [the meaning of the saying] "Mr. Zhang drinks wine and Mr. Li gets drunk." This is the perfect time to come to my gate to get a beating.

Why? Because you still have to break through the double barrier of the ancestral teachers of Zen. You still have to visit all the men of knowledge, and find out which ones are shallow and which ones are deep.

Then you must come back to [a secluded place] at the seaside or in the forest, and protect and nurture the embryo of sagehood until the nagas and devas push you forward. Only then can you come forward to uphold the teaching of the Zen school and save all sentient beings.

Instructions from Master Xueting

Twenty-four hours a day, with no other distractions, contemplate [the koan]: "Before my father and mother were born, what was my original face?"
Do not concern yourself with whether or not you gain power, or whether or not oblivion and scattering set in. Just keep your attention focussed [on this koan].

Instructions from Zen teacher Zhengyou of Ancient Plum Temple on Mount Yangshan [1285-1352]

You must generate a brave and bold attitude, and firmly establish your resolve your resolve to take all that you have understood and learned throughout your whole life, all your knowledge of the Buddhism and its various writings, and your samadhi of words, and sweep it into the sea, and pay no further attention to it.

Take your eighty-four thousand subtle thoughts and cut them off. In their place, take the koan that is your basic study, and bring it to your attention. Keep on doubting and doubting and pressing and pressing. Concentrate your body and mind and seek insight. Make enlightenment your standard.

Do not try to figure and calculate from the koans, or seek and search from the texts of the scriptures. You simply must break with this [intellectual approach] abruptly, and cut it off sharply. Only then will you arrive home.

If you cannot keep your attention on the koan, try three times in succession to focus on it. Then you will feel there is power.

[While you are sitting in meditation], if your physical strength is exhausted, or if your mind is full of melancholy, then casually get up and walk around a bit. Then return to the meditation cushion, and come to grips as before with the koan that you are studying.

If you begin to fall asleep as soon as you sit on the meditation cushion; if you are able to keep your eyes open, and your thoughts are chaotic and confused; if you get up and walk around and repeatedly bend your ear to listen to what people are saying out loud and whispering; if you remember a belly full of Zen sayings and scriptural texts and show off your eloquence–if you use your mind like this, when the last day of your life arrives, all [your efforts to "study Zen"] will have been to no avail.

From Zen teacher Jiefeng Shiyu [1301-1370]
(to Lecturer Shan of Mount Wutai)

Even if Manjushri [the bodhisattva of transcendent wisdom] emits a golden light and rubs your head and lets you ride his lion, even if Guanyin [the bodhisattva of infinite compassion] reveals her thousand hands and eyes and lets us hold her oriole, all of this is pursuing form and sound: what good does it do your true self?

If you want to illuminate your own great affair [of enlightenment], and penetrate through the barrier of birth and death, first you must cut off all vain and false interpretations of ordinary and holy. Twenty-four hours a day, turn the light around and reflect back. Just contemplate [the koan] "It is not buddha, it is not mind, it is not things: what is it?"

Do not seek [for the answer to this] outside yourself. If there is the slightest particle of 'Buddha Dharma', 'supernatural powers', or 'sagely understanding', you have deceived yourself. All [such reified concepts amount to] slandering the Buddha and the Dharma.

You must study until your are totally independent, relying on nothing and positing nothing.

When you can focus the eye [of enlightenment], you will see [the meaning of koans like [these]:

"What is the Buddha Dharma?"–"A cloth shirt from Qingzhou."

and

"Did you meet [Zen master] Nanquan in person or not?"–"In [the region of] Zhenzhou the turnips are big."

All [such Zen koans] will be tools you use in your own home. You will not have to search any more for supernatural powers or sagely understanding.

Reply to the Emperor by Zen teacher Lingyin Huitang [1103-1176]

The Song Emperor Xiaozong [r. 1163-1189] asked: "How can one avoid birth and death?"

Lingyin replied: "One will never be able to avoid birth and death without awakening to the Great Vehicle Path."

The Emperor also asked: "How can one awaken to it?"

Lingyin said: "All those who over the months and years polish the true nature they inherently possess will awaken to it."

Instructions from Master Puyan Duan-an of Dasheng Mountain

"The myriad things return to one: what does the one return to?"

You should not sit preserving empty stillness without contemplating a koan. You should not sit mindful of the koan without doubting it.

If there is oblivion or scattering, do not arouse thought to banish it: quickly put your attention on the koan, arouse body and mind, and boldly apply your energy.

If it still is not right, get up and walk around, and when you feel the oblivion or scattering depart, go back to the meditation cushion.

Suddenly your attention stays on [the koan] spontaneously without you having to direct it, and your doubt continues by itself without you having to make yourself doubt.

You walk without being aware you are walking and sit without being aware you are sitting. All that's there is the feeling of studying [the koan], alone and clear and distinct and bright. This is the place where affliction is cut off and where the [conditioned] self is lost.

Even if it is like this, this is not yet the ultimate. Urge yourself on ever more, and contemplate "Where does the one return to?"

When you reach this level, there are no longer any stages or steps for keeping your attention on the koan. There is only the feeling of doubt. If you forget it, immediately bring it up again. When the mind that is reflecting back is exhausted, this is called "phenomena forgotten": only with this do you reach the place of no-mind, [the stage where the conditioned mind of delusion no longer prevails].

Isn't this the ultimate? An ancient said, "Do not think that no-mind is the Path. No-mind is still separated [from the Path] by one more barrier layer." Suddenly you bump into it while encountering sound and form: you give a great laugh, and your existence has been transformed. Then you may well say, 'The ox in Huaizhou eats grain, and the horse in Yizhou gets fat'."

Instructions to the assembly by Guzhuo

O virtuous ones, why don't you arouse a great zeal to progress, and undertake a great vow before the Buddha, Dharma, and Sangha, swearing not to leave the mountain until you illuminate birth and death and penetrate through the barrier of the ancestral teachers?

Hang up your bowl and bag by the meditation bench. [As you sit in meditation], tower up like a mile-high wall and get to the bottom of this birth, penetrate all the way through. If you discern this mind [of enlightenment], you surely will not be deceived.

There are those whose aspiration [for enlightenment] is not genuine, and whose will is not bold and sharp. They pass the winter here and the summer there –they go forward today and fall back tomorrow. Having searched for a long time without finding anything, they claim that transcendent wisdom has no spiritual efficacy.

Then they go outside [Buddhism] to write out a record of their belly full [of disillusioned impressions], like a jar of stinking dregs. Those who hear [them talk] cannot but feel loathing and vomit. They may go on writing [in this vein] until [the remote future when] Maitreya is born on earth, but what does this have to do with [the Buddha Dharma]? How painful!

Instructions from Zen teacher Taixu

If you have not yet completely awakened, you must go to the meditation cushion and sit impassively for ten, twenty, thirty years, observing your original face before your father and mother were born.

Instructions from Zen teacher Chushi Fanqi [1296-1370]

Brothers [and sisters], some people claim to be Zen followers, but when we ask them what Zen is, they look back and forth and their mouths are pulled down into a frown. How painful! How wrong! They are eating the food of the buddhas and patriarchs, but they do not go on to try to understand the fundamental matter [of enlightenment]. They compete to memorize literary language and vulgar phrases, making a lot of noise, without the least bit of hesitancy or any feeling of shame.

Some do not go to the meditation cushion to investigate their original face before their father and mother were born. [Instead], they stay on the sidelines, learning

to be hired rice-pounders, hoping to find merit and re-
pent and remove karmic obstructions. They are very far
indeed from the Path.

[Some people hold the opinion that the way to
study Zen is] to freeze the mind and rein in thoughts, to
gather in things and return them to emptiness. As soon
as a thought arises, they immediately try to block it.
[People with] this kind of view are outsiders who have
fallen into empty annihilation, dead people whose souls
have not returned.

There is another type who wrongly accept [as true
nature] the subjective ability to get angry and feel happy,
to see and hear. They think that when they have clearly
recognized this, their life's work of study is completed.

I would ask them: Where does the one who is able
to get angry and feel happy, to see and hear, go to when
impermanence arrives, and you are burnt into a pile of
ashes?

What is learned like this is "imitation-silver Zen."
This "silver" is not real: once it is heated up, it immediately [melts and] runs off.

[With this type] I ask, "What do you usually study?"

They answer, "We have been taught to study [the
koan] 'The myriad things return to one: where does the
one return to?' And we have been taught to understand
just like this [that our subjectivity is our true nature].
Only today have we found out [from you] that this is
wrong. We have come to you, Master, to ask for a koan."

I tell them, "There is nothing wrong in the koans of
the ancients. Your eye is fundamentally correct. You
have gone wrong because of your teachers."

If they persist in asking [for a koan], I tell them, "Go
study the koan 'A dog has no buddha-nature.' When

suddenly you smash the lacquer bucket [of ignorance], come back into my hands and get a beating."

Zhuhong's comment:

From Tianru on, all [the Zen teachers quoted above] were experienced adepts from the period from the end of the Yuan dynasty to the first years of our own [Ming] dynasty. As for Jiefeng, Guzhuo, and Chushi, their lives spanned both periods.

Chushi was the fifth generation descendant of Miaoxi [the illustrious Song dynasty Zen master Dahui Zonggao]. Chushi's perception was as bright and clear as the sun and moon, and his eloquence was as sharp and swift as thunder and wind. He cut straight through to the root-source and sloughed off the branches and leaves. He truly was no embarrassment to Miaoxi.

From [the time of] Tianru until the present, there has been no one to match [Chushi]. In what they say [the teachers since then] only mention matters of the ultimate paradigm of transcendence. Very few of them teach beginning students how to do meditation work. The one or two [recent examples of concrete lessons on how to meditate] which I have found are recorded below.

Letter from the Korean Zen teacher Pogye in answer to Prime Minister Yi

Since you have already focussed your attention on the koan "No", you do not have to change your study. When you focus on any other koan, since you have already studied the koan "No", you are sure to have a causal basis with the koan "No" that is a bit ripe.

It is important that you do not shift or change your study.

Just keep your attention on the koan twenty-four hours a day, whatever you are doing. It does not matter how long it takes until you awaken or do not awaken.

Do not concern yourself with whether it is flavorful or flavorless. Do not concern yourself with whether you get power or not. Press on to where thoughts do not reach, to where thoughts do not operate. This is where all the buddhas and ancestral teachers put down their bodies and lives.

Zhuhong's comment:

A record of this letter was obtained from Korea in 1597 by Xu Yuanzhen of Fujian in his eastern expedition: it was not extant in China. I have edited it to record its important parts.

Talks by Zen master Chushan Shaoqi at the end of the summer retreat

O virtuous ones, in this ninety day period [of the summer retreat], have you experienced awakening or not?

If you have not yet awakened, then this winter will also be lost to no avail.

If you are genuine people of the Path, then you take [all the timespans of] all the worlds in the universe as your time limit for perfect enlightenment. It does not matter [if you have to practice] for a long period or for a short period, for a hundred days or a thousand days, whether starting a retreat or ending a retreat: you just start by focusing your attention on a koan.

If you do not awaken in one year, you study for another year. If you do not awaken in ten years, you study for another ten years. If you do not awaken in twenty years, you study for another twenty years. If you you go through your whole life without awakening, you certainly do not alter your purpose. You must see the real ultimate: only then can you put aside your studies.

If you are not yet able to get the message before words, just take the phrase "Amitabha Buddha" and hold it in your heart. Silently investigate it, and constantly whip up your feelings of doubt about "Who is this one reciting the buddha-name?"

Let your recitation be continuous, and your mindfulness unbroken. It is like being a person travelling along a road: when you reaches the place where the rivers and mountains end, naturally there is a truth there that transforms your existence.

Zhuhong's comment:

Putting your attention on the koan is the stage where you enter. [Witnessing] the real ultimate is the stage where you emerge. Fix this securely in your memory.

Instructions from Zen teacher Tianzhen Dufeng

If in fact you want complete liberation from birth and death, first you must develop the mind of great faith and undertake far-reaching vows.

Swear that if you do not smash through the koan you are studying and clearly see your original face from before your father and mother were born, you will not abandon the koan that is your fundamental study.

Swear that you will not leave your genuine enlightened teacher to pursue fame and profit. Swear that you will descend into the evil planes [of hell-beings, hungry ghosts, and animals] if you go against this vow.

Only when you have taken this great vow, and fortified your mind, are you qualified to take on a koan.

If you contemplate the koan "No", the crucial thing is to apply effort to [the koan] "Why does a dog have no buddha-nature?"

If you contemplate [the koan] "The myriad things return to one", the crucial thing lies in "Where does the one return to?"

If you investigate reciting the buddha-name, the crucial thing lies in "Who is the one reciting the buddha-name?"

[Whatever the koan you study], turn the light around and reflect back. Deeply enter into the feeling of doubt.

If you do not get power from the koan, focus your attention on it again from beginning to end, and unify it from head to tail: then at last you will have a starting point to arouse doubt. With the feeling of doubt unbroken, apply your mind to [the koan] most urgently.

When you take a step without realizing it and transform your existence, turning a somersault into the void, come back to me again to get a beating.

Instructions from Zen teacher Konggu Jinglong [b. 1392]

You should not act stupid and dull while mindful of the koan. Nor should you ponder it in detail and try to figure it out.

Just be adamant all the time, intent on illuminating this matter [of enlightenment]. Suddenly while hanging from the cliff, you will let go, and transform your existence. Only then will you see the solitary light shining clear.

When you reach this point, you must not sink into it. There is still the hammerblow to the back of the head. It is extremely difficult to pass through. You should just keep on studying this way.

In high antiquity there were cases of spontaneous enlightenment without study. Since then, there have been no cases of attaining enlightenment without putting effort into study.

Master Youtan directed you to focus on "Who is the one reciting the buddha-name?" Now you do not have to use this method any more. Just go on as usual reciting [the buddha-name]: just be mindful [of buddha constantly] without forgetting.

Suddenly as you encounter objects, you will achieve the phrase that transforms your existence. Only then will you realize that the Pure Land of silent light is not apart from this place here, and that Amitabha Buddha is not beyond your own mind.

Zhuhong's comment:

"Just be adamant all the time, intent on illuminating this matter." This sentence is very wondrous. It fully encompasses all the intricacies of the method of contemplating koans.

Instructions from Master Tianqi

Right now generate a firm decision to keep your attention fixed on [the koan] that is your fundamental study for three days and three nights: resolve to see what truth it is. Insist on finding clear comprehension.

[If you do this] oblivion will retreat spontaneously without having to be refined away, and scattering will be cut off spontaneously without having to be cleared away. [Your concentration] will be pure and unmixed: thoughts will not be born.

Suddenly you will understand as if waking up from a dream. Keep on contemplating [the koan] as before: everything is empty and illusory in its essence, fundamentally appearing ready-made. The dense array of myriad images [is] the whole appearing alone.

[After you have witnessed this] it will not be in vain that you are a person in this land of China, it will not be in vain that you are a monk in this Dharma-Gate. You will pass your days going back and forth following circumstances: won't you be happy and content!

You recite the buddha-name all day long, but you do not realize that it is entirely buddha doing the reciting.

If you don't know this, you must contemplate [the koan] "Who is the one reciting the buddha-name?" Then your eyes will look upon it steadily, and your mind will focus upon it steadily. You must find out where it comes down.

Zhuhong's comment:

Dufeng and Tianqi both taught people to study buddha-name recitation. Why did [their contemporary]

Konggu say it is not necessary to use this method? Because the way they [as teachers] accorded with [students'] potentials was not the same, and they went along with what was expedient without obstruction.

Instructions from Zen teacher Guyin Jingqin

The good and bad [visions] that appear to you as you are sitting [in meditation] are entirely due to the fact that when you are sitting, you do not arouse your [power of] observation and do not properly adjust your contemplation.

You just sit quietly with your eyes shut, without generating mental energy, your thoughts flowing along following objects, half dreaming and half awake. You may crave the quietude as pleasurable, and make all sorts of mental states and visionary scenes appear.

In doing the meditation work that is the true basis [for enlightenment], when you have to sleep, you sleep. As soon as you wake up, you arouse your energy, rub your eyes, clench your teeth, curl your hands into fists, and directly observe the koan to see what it really means. It is important not to sink into oblivion and torpor. If there is the slightest external object, you should not grasp it.

Whether you are walking, standing, sitting, or lying down, do not let [your mindfulness] of the phrase "Amitabha Buddha" be interrupted.

You must be confident that when the causal basis is profound, the result will be profound. Make yourself mindful [of "Amitabha Buddha"] spontaneously without [having to deliberately] recite it. If you can be continuously mindful of it, without any gaps, I guarantee your mindfulness will fuse into a single whole [with the buddha-name].

In the midst of your mindfulness, you will recognize the person who is mindful: then Amitabha and you will appear together.

From the *Resolving Doubts Collection* by Zen teacher Deng of Yiyan

Question: When the students study with teachers, some teachers direct them to keep their attention on the koan, and some direct them to doubt the koan. Are these the same or different?

Answer: As soon as you put your attention on a koan, you immediately doubt it. How could there be two principles here? As soon as your attention is focused, the feeling of doubt appears. When you keep on going over and over it, energetically investigating it and delving into it, so that your work deepens and your effort peaks, you naturally attain complete awakening.

Zhuhong's comment:

This passage from the *Resolving Doubts Collection* is the finest and most fitting. Contemporary students often get stuck regarding these two points and cannot decide. This is because they have not really done meditation work.

Instructions from Master Yuexin

Vigorously generate a renewed intent and energy, and focus on the koan.

You must let your feeling of doubt rest for a long time on the concluding words, and let it deepen and become acute.

You may grapple with the koan silently with your mouth shut, or you may pursue your investigation of the koan letting your voice come forth.

[When studying the koan, you should feel] as if you have lost something important. You must personally encounter it and personally recover it. Think of nothing else [but the koan] at any time, wherever you are in the course of your daily activities.

II. Brief Stories of the Labors of the Ancestral Teachers

Sitting alone in a quiet room

The great teacher Dao-an [312-385] sat alone in a quiet room for twelve years, exerting his spirit to the utmost in contemplation: only then did he attain spiritual awakening.

Sitting in a tree hanging over a cliff

Zen teacher Jinglin gave up lecturing on the sutras to practice Zen, but drowsiness disturbed his mind.

There was a precipitous cliff with a thousand foot drop, with a tree projecting out over it. Jinglin tied himself to this tree with a rope of plaited straw, and sat crosslegged in the treetop. He wholeheartedly focused his mind, and [sat there] day and night. Such was his fear of death [in such a precarious position], that he was able to concentrate his spirit singlemindedly. Later he experienced transcendent awakening.

Staying in the woods and living on herbs

Zen teacher Tongda went into the Great White Mountains. He had no supply of grain, so when he was hungry, he ate herbs. He rested under the trees. He sat upright contemplating the mystery for five years without stopping.

Once he happened to hit a clump of dirt with a stick, and when the clump of dirt broke up, he opened up in great enlightenment.

Never loosening the belt of the garment

Zen teacher Zhao of Golden Light Temple left home when he was thirteen. At nineteen he went to Hongyang Mountain and took refuge with Master Jiaye. He served him diligently for three years. He never loosened the belt of his garment, and when he slept he never lay down. He was still conducting himself like this when he opened up and was enlightened at Mount Gushe.

Pricking oneself with an awl

Ciming [987-1040], Guquan, and Langye were comrades when they studied with Fenyang [947-1024]. At the time it was bitter cold in [that region of China,] Hedong, and it was causing the congregation much distress.Ciming's intent was set on the Path, and he never forgot it day or night. When he felt sleepy as he was sitting at night, he would take an awl and prick himself [to stay awake]. Later he became Fenyang's successor and greatly energized the wind of the Path. He was called the "Lion of West River".

Sitting in a dark room without becoming inattentive.

At first Zen teacher Hongzhi [1091-1157] was the attendant of Chun of Danxia.

Once, when Hongzhi was inquiring about a koan with some other monks, he unknowingly laughed out loud.

Chun scolded him saying, "How many good things you have lost by this laugh! Haven't you seen the saying, 'If you are absent even for a moment, you are the same as a dead man'?"

Hongzhi bowed in homage and took [what Chun said] to heart. Thereafter even when he was in a dark room he never dared to be inattentive.

Weeping in the night

Zen teacher Quan of Yi-an [d. 1180] was very sharp in his work. [Every day] when it got late he was sure to start weeping and think to himself, "Another day I have passed in vain like this. I wonder how my work will go tomorrow."

When Quan was in the congregation of monks, he never exchanged a single word with anyone.

Three years of energetic practice

Zen master Zuxin of Huitang [1025-1100] would say of himself, "When I first entered the Path, it was very easy to go my own way. Then when I met my late teacher Huanglong, I reflected back on my daily activities and saw that there were many many contradictions [between my conduct] and the principles [of the Buddhist Path]. So I practiced [the Path] energetically for three years, through the bitter cold and stifling heat, without wavering from my true intent. Only then did I get so that everything was in accord with the principles [of the Path]. Now even when I cough and spit or shrug my shoulders, it is all the essential meaning the Zen transmission.

A round headrest to prevent dozing off

Attendant Zhe [d. 1095] used a round piece of wood as a headrest. When he began to doze off, the headrest would roll, and he would be awakened and get up again. He did this most of the time and made it his constant practice. Someone said to him that he was overtaxing his mind, but he answered: "My affinity with transcendent wisdom is slight: if I do not act like this, I am afraid I will be dragged off by false habits."

Standing in the rain without noticing it

Hermit Fen was full of zeal for the Path. He had no spare time to eat or rest.

One day as he was leaning on the balustrade contemplating [the koan] "Does a dog have buddha-nature or not?"–"No," it started to rain, but he did not notice. Only when his robe got soaked did he realize [it had been raining].

Vowing not to spread out the coverlet

Zen teacher Shouxun of Buddha Lamp Temple was a disciple of Fojian. He went to follow the congregation [into the hall] to ask for instruction, but it was crowded and there was no room for him. He lamented, "If I do not get total realization in this life, I swear never to spread out my coverlet [to sleep]."   From then on, he stood there leaning against a pillar for forty-nine days, as if mourning for his dead mother, until he attained great enlightenment.

Throwing away books

[At the beginning of his Zen studies] Tiemian Zhibing went travelling on foot. Not long after he left his home village, he noticed that the fire from his ordination ceremony the night before was still smoldering: it had all come down to a few last embers in the brazier.

He took his books and threw them on the ground saying, "These confuse a person's conceptual mind in vain."

A firm pledge to develop insight

When Zen teacher Lingyuan Weiqing [d. 1117] was first studying with Huanglong Zuxin, he went with the congregation [to hear] a question and answer session. He was totally confused and did not have a clue.

That night he made a vow before [an image of]

Buddha: "Till the end of my life, I will make the Dharma my mission. I vow to understand it as soon as possible."

Later he was reading the sayings of [Zen Master] Xuansha. He became tired and leaned against a wall. Then he got up to walk around. He was walking quickly and one of his shoes fell off: when he reached down to get it, he was greatly enlightened.

Never any other object

Zen teacher Yuanwu Keqin [1063-1135] studied many times with Wuzu Fayan of East Mountain. When he was Fayan's attendant, he exerted himself to the utmost studying. He said to himself, "While I am in this congregation, I will never have any other object of concern [than to reach enlightenment]." After ten years he finally penetrated all the way through.

Never forgetting even while busy

Zen teacher Mu-an Fazhong [1084-1149] at first studied the Tiantai Buddhist philosophy. Later he became intent on the Zen school, and visited Longmen Yan.

Even when he was busy, he never forgot to keep his attention [on his meditation]. Once as he was working the treadmill on the water wheel, he happened to look at the temple signboard, which said, "The wheel of the Dharma is always turning." Suddenly he was greatly enlightened.

Oblivious of reaching the ford

Zen teacher Qingshou Jiaoheng studied with Master Bao of Universal Awareness Temple in Zhengzhou. He worked assiduously day and night.

One day he went on an errand to [the town of] Suiyang. As he passed through Zhao Ford, his feeling of doubt [about the koan he was studying] had not dissipated, and he was oblivious that he had reached the ford. His travelling companions alerted him and said, "This is the ford in the river." Jiaoheng opened up: sadness and joy were mingled.

When he told Master Bao about this, the Master said, "This stiff corpse is still not there." So he directed Jiaoheng to study the saying about the Sun Face Buddha. [The temple superintendent asked Mazu, "How is your health lately, Master?" Mazu said, "Sun Face Buddha, Moon Face Buddha."]

One day while Heng was sitting quietly in the Cloud Hall, he was greatly enlightened as he heard the sound of the board [being struck].

Forgetting sleep and food

Zen teacher Yue of Songyuan [1132-1202] studied first as a layman with Hua of Ying-an, but he did not reach accord with him.

He spurred himself on even more, and went to see Jie of Mi-an, who answered whatever he asked. Mi-an sighed and said, "This is only cut and dried Zen."

Yue's efforts became even more intense, to the point that he forgot to sleep or eat. It so happened that Mi-an was in his private room questioning a monk [about the koan], "It is not mind, it is not buddha, it is not things: what is it?"

Yue, who was standing by his side, was greatly enlightened.

Forgetting mouth and body

When Zen teacher Gaofeng Yuanmiao [1238-1295] was in the congregation [of monks, before he was a teacher], his side never touched his mat [because he never lay down]. He forgot both his mouth and his body. Sometimes when he had to go to the toilet, he left [the meditation hall] still in the robe [worn only for meditating]. Sometimes he went out without fastening his garment in back. Later on, as he was returning to the meditation hall at Jingshan Temple, he had his great enlightenment.

Ending all entanglements

Zen teacher Shiyu of Jiefeng [1301-1370] studied first with Guyan and Shimen, and took their teaching words to heart. He sat impassively day and night, but he did not reach accord [with Reality]..

Later he studied with Zhiyan, [who directed him] to focus on [the koan] "It is not mind, it is not buddha, it is not things." He felt more and more doubt until all entanglements ended. He was oblivious of sleep and food, like someone whose vital breath has been cut off.

One night Shiyu had been sitting in meditation until midnight, when he heard one of the nearby monks reciting the [passage in] the *Song of Enlightenment* which says: "Do not remove false thoughts and do not seek the real". He suddenly emptied through: it was as if a heavy burden had melted away.

He spoke a verse:

> Face to face all the time, we never met
> Having totally exhausted the energy my mama
>   bore me with
> At midnight I suddenly forget the moon and the
>   pointing finger
> From the emptiness the sun's disc comes forth
>   red

Shutting the door and studying energetically

State Minister Yi Cizhen studied with old man Wansong [1166-1246]. He put aside his family duties, and cut off his contacts with people. Despite the bitter cold and stifling heat, he did not miss a day of study. For almost three years he studied day and night, heedless of sleeping and eating, until he finally got the realization that sealed him [as enlightened].

Zhuhong's comment:

One who employs mind like this and realizes the Path like this is called a "householder bodhisattva." What good does it do to eat your fill of meat, and then come looking for a monk to talk about Zen?

Leaning the head against a pillar

[While still a student], Zen teacher Zhongfeng Mingben [1263-1323] was the attendant of Siguan of

Gaofeng. He worked hard day and night. When he got tired, he would lean his head against a pillar.

One day he was reciting the Diamond Sutra. When he reached the passage about carrying the Tathagata, he had a sudden understanding. He thought to himself, "This is not yet the ultimate realization," and carried on working even more assiduously, tirelessly seeking certainty. Later, while he was observing water flow, he was greatly enlightened.

Zhuhong's comment:

Because he thought to himself, "What I have realized is not yet the ultimate", in the end he reached the ultimate. These days, alas, there are many who think being on the road is arriving home.

Austerities at the barrier

Zen teacher Dufeng Benshan [1419-1482] sojourned at the [toll] barrier at Yuqi. He did not set up a bed, but just a stool [with the intention of sitting in meditation all the time and never lying down to sleep]. He made enlightenment his standard.

One night he was very sleepy, and without his noticing it, it got to be midnight. [Thereafter] he got off the stool and spent his days and nights walking and standing.

Once he fell asleep leaning against a wall, so he swore not to get near any walls. He walked up and down in the covered walkway until his physical strength was exhausted. The demon of sleep weighed on him more and more. He wept and wailed in front of [the statue of buddha], assailed by a hundred pains.

Later he got to where his meditation work progressed day by day. [Suddenly one day] when he heard the sound of a bell, he [encountered fundamental reality, and] he was not on his own [anymore].

His enlightenment verse went like this:

> Profoundly silent, utterly still, without any
> doings
> As I touch it, for no reason I roar like thunder
> With a sound that moves the earth, the scene
> ends
> My skull is pulverized, and the dream returns

Ribs never touching the mat

Zen teacher Jin of Jade Peak studied with Hai of Jinyun. Hai taught him the koan "The myriad things return to one: where does the one return to?"

Jin was in doubt about this for three years. Once, when he happened to be picking vegetables, Jin suddenly solidified and stayed that way for a long time.

Hai asked him, "Are you stabilized?"

Jin said, "Whether I am stabilized or in motion does not matter."

Hai said, "Who is it for whom being stabilized or in motion does not matter?"

Jin took a basket and showed it to Hai. Hai did not approve. Jin knocked the basket to the ground, but Hai still did not approve.

After this, Jin's meditation work became more and more urgent. His ribs did not touch his mat [because he never lay down] and he would sit [meditating] for seven days at a stretch. One day he heard the sound of someone chopping wood and was greatly enlightened.

Persisting in dull meditation work

When Zen teacher Wuji of Western Shu was first doing meditation work, he would not even look at little slips of paper with anything written on them. He just went on like a blind man doing dull meditation work, and finally he achieved great penetration and great enlightenment.

Zhuhong's comment:

The idea behind this is very correct. But those who do not clearly understand the principles of the teaching should not 'imitate the wrinkles' [by acting dull because they do not know any better].

III. Citations from the Scriptures

The Great Perfection of Wisdom Sutra [j. 88]:

From the sky came a voice telling the Bodhisattva
Sadapralapa ['he who is always weeping' for suffering
sentient beings]: "When you travel east seeking transcendent wisdom, do not give up when you are tired, do not
care when you feel sleepy, do not be concerned with
food and drink, pay no attention to whether it is day or
night, do not fear heat or cold, do not let your mind
scatter in confusion over internal or external phenomena, do not notice what is to your right or to your left, do
not look up or down or east or west or north or south."

The Flower Ornament Scripture [ch. 10, "A
Bodhisattva Asks for Clarification"]:

The Bodhisattva Qinshou said in verse:
    It is like drilling for fire [with a firedrill and bow]
    If you stop [drilling] before [the fire appears]
    The impetus to fire immediately ceases
    The lazy ones are like this too
A commentary explains: "You must use wisdom to bore
in and focus on a single objective. Use expedient means
as the string [of the bow] to turn [the 'firedrill' of wisdom]
skillfully. When the mind's wisdom does not stop, and
[your 'drilling' effort] is uninterrupted whatever you are
doing, then the holy path can be born. If [ordinary
states of] mind arise even for an instant, or you momen-
tarily forget your awareness [of your objective], this
means you are stopping.

The Moon Treasury Scripture:

If you can work assiduously and fix your mindfulness so that it does not scatter, then you will put an end to affliction, and achieve supreme enlightenment.

The Scripture of the Sixteen Contemplations of Amitabha:

Buddha told Princess Vaideshi: "You must concentrate your mind, and focus your attention."

The Emergence of the Sunlight Scripture:

Intelligent people use wisdom to refine mind and put an end to defilements.

It is like putting ore [into the furnace] many times to be refined over and over again: then it becomes pure metal.

It is like the great ocean swirling back and forth day and night until a great pearl is formed.

People are like this too. If they work on their minds day and night without stopping, then they will achieve realization.

Zhuhong's comment:

People these days only know how to stop their minds and enter into meditation. They do not know how to work on mind and achieve realization.

The Great Anointing Scripture:

Meditating monks have no other thoughts: they keep to one dharma, and later they see Mind.

The Bequeathed Teaching Scripture:

As for mind, focus it in one place, and everything will be accomplished.

Zhuhong's comment:

"Keep to one dharma", "focus it in once place"—how lucky we are to have such sayings!

The Heroic March Scripture:

Make a refined investigation this mind inside and out. Take this mind and investigate it until it is totally purified and refined to its essence.

The Amitabha Scripture:

Hold to the buddha-name, so that mind is unified and does not scatter.

Zhuhong's comment:

The task of Zen is completed [when you attain the state described by] this line "mind is unified and does not scatter."

People often overlook this [and wrongly imagine that Pure Land and Zen do not have the same goal].

The Scripture of the Descent into Lanka:

If you want complete knowledge of subject and object and the realms of discrimination, they are all things made manifest by mind. You must detach from anger and confusion and stagnation and torpor and drowsiness and sleep, and work hard day and night cultivating practice.

The Diamond Wisdom Scripture:

The bodhisattva Sadapralapa went for seven years walking and standing without ever sitting or lying down.

The Heap of Jewels Scripture:

Buddha told Shariputra, "When these two bodhisattvas were in their period of energetic advance, they went for a thousand years without being harried by sleepiness for even a moment.

"In a thousand years they never thought to judge whether their food was tasty or bland or good or bad.

"In a thousand years, whenever they were begging for food, they never looked to see if the person giving the food was a man or a woman.

"For a thousand years they lived under the trees without every looking up to see what the trees looked liked.

"For a thousand years they never thought of their homes or families.

"For a thousand years they never thought, 'I want to shave my head.'

"For a thousand years they never thought to try to get cool when it was hot or to try to get warm when it was cold.

"For a thousand years they never talked of worldly things of no benefit."

The Great Collection Scripture:

The monk 'Dharma-Awakening' constantly practiced buddha-name recitation for twenty thousand years without sleeping and without engendering craving or anger. He gave no thought to his kinfolk, to clothing or food, or to anything to support his physical existence.

The Scripture on Concentration via Buddha-Remembrance

For twenty years, Shariputra scrupulously cultivated his practice of *vipashyana* [insight meditation] all the time: whether walking, standing, sitting, or lying down, he contemplating [everything] with correct mindfulness, and never wavered or fell into confusion.

The Scripture of the Bodhisattva 'Sovereign King':

[When the bodhisattva 'Sovereign King' was still in his incarnation as] the monk Jingangqi, and was cultivating his practice of the Correct Dharma, various demons waited by his side in concealment. They waited by his side for a thousand years, but they never saw a moment when his mind scattered, in which they could have disturbed him.

The Tathagata's Seal of Wisdom Scripture:

The universal monarch Huiqi abandoned his kingdom and left home. For three thousand years he focused his mind and never lay down.

The Middle Agama:

The venerable ones Aniruddha, Nandi, and Khumbira were staying together in the forest. After going out to beg for food, they would return to sit in meditation. When dawn came, they would get up from their [meditation] seats, and draw water [to wash]. If one of them could manage, he would carry [the water] by himself, but if he could not lift it, he would beckon with his hand to one of the other monks, and the two of them would carry it together. They never spoke with each other. Once every five days, they would preach the Dharma together, or keep a holy silence.

Zhuhong's comment:

Through the generations this has been an excellent model for forming associations to cultivate practice.

The Scripture of Various Parables:

In the land of Varanasi [in India], a man left home.
He swore to himself never to lie down to rest until he
had achieved accord with reality. Day and night he kept
walking, and after three years he attained enlightenment.

In the land of Rajagrha [in India], there was a monk
who spread out straw as a mat and sat upon it, vowing
never to get up until he attained the Path. When he was
drowsy, he would pierce his thigh with an awl. Within
one year, he reached accord with the True Path.

The Mixed Agama:

Monks like this work assiduously with skillful
means, and do not forsake good dharmas even if they
become emaciated from hunger and their bones stick
out under their skin.

As long as they do not attain what they must attain,
they do not abandon their energetic progress: the always
rein in their minds, and do not allow self-indulgence.

Zhuhong's comment:

"What they must attain"–[this phrase in the scripture implies of course that] one must know what it is that
must be attained.

According to this scripture [which belongs to the
Lesser Vehicle], what must be attained is: to end all defilements; to experience the three understandings [of
past lives, of future events, and of the ending of afflic-
tion] and the six supernatural powers [to see everything,
to hear everything, to read minds, to know past lives, to

travel anywhere unimpeded, to transform things]; and to attain the fruits of the *shravakas* [the 'hearers', the followers of the lesser vehicle, the vehicle of individual salvation].

What we aim for now [in the Greater Vehicle], is to attain complete enlightenment to the mind-source, to experience omniscience, and to attain the supreme fruit of buddhahood.

The Agama:

To achieve the three knowledges and eliminate darkness and confusion and attain the clarity of great wisdom: all this is brought about by scrupulously cultivating practice, living in stillness and solitude, and ceaselessly concentrating mindfulness.

Zhuhong's comment:

If you concentrate your mind ceaselessly for a long time, mind will be unified and freed from confusion.

Essential Verses from the Dharma Collection:

If for a hundred years a person is lazy and neglects energetic progress, it is not as good as a single day of the bold practice of energetic progress.

Zhuhong's comment:

If you recognize the meaning of this, then you will have no doubts at all about cases like the butcher who feared for the karmic retribution for all the killing he had done, and invited a monk to recite the buddha-name on his behalf, and subsequently went to the Pure Land, and you will have no doubts about the concept of achieving birth in the Pure Land due to ten [utterly sincere] recitations of the buddha-name at the moment of death.

The Infinite Life Scripture:

If with perfect sincerity you strive energetically to make progress, and you seek the Path ceaselessly, you will certain get the results, and all your vows will be fulfilled.

The Scripture of the Bodhisattva 'Ever Being Born':

In ancient times, when Amitabha Buddha was a prince, he learned of this subtle wondrous teaching. He faithfully upheld it and made energetic progress. For seven thousand years, his side never touched his mat and his intent never wavered.

The Jewel Heap Correct Teaching Scripture:

Those who enjoy seeking the Great Vehicle have minds that are bold and brave. Even if they have to give up their bodies and their lives, they do not mind. They cultivate the practices of bodhisattvas, and work hard to increase their energy and progress. They are not the least bit lazy.

The Six Perfections Scripture:

The infinite perfection of energetic progress means focusing your energy on the mystery of the Path, and tirelessly making progress towards it. Whether you are lying down, sitting, standing, or walking, you never slack off even for a moment.

The Scripture on the Stages of Cultivating the Path:

Buddha said: "When you see your past lives, you will see that you have being going back and forth through birth and death for countless eons. [With all the bodies you have had] your bones [would make a pile] higher than the polar mountain; your marrow would cover the ground of all the worlds in the galaxy; your blood would be more than all the rains that have fallen everywhere on earth from past to present.

"If you wish to avoid the travail of all this birth and death, make energetic progress day and night, and seek the uncontrived [absolute reality]."

Zhuhong's comment:

[In the passages above we read such phrases as] "Seek the Path," "Hear this subtle wondrous teaching," "Enjoy seeking the Great Vehicle," "Focus energy on the mystery of the Path," and "Seek the uncontrived [absolute reality]."

To make energetic progress like this is called correct energetic progress. Otherwise, even if you tire out your body and will in strenuous austerities for years and for eons, you sink down among the outside paths, or you fall into the one-sided vehicles, and it will never do any good.

The Basic Practice of Bodhisattvas Scripture:

Going on to achieve buddhahood all depends on energetic progress.

The Questions of Maitreya Scripture:

Buddha said to Ananda: "Maitreya generated his will [for enlightenment] forty-two eons before me. I generated the will for enlightenment after him, but I passed through nine eons with energetic progress, and attained true supreme enlightenment [before him]."

Zhuhong's comment:

Shakyamuni Buddha began his advance later, and overtook one who had started forty-two eons earlier. This was brought about by the difference between working hard and being lazy.

The scriptures judged this by saying that the reason Maitreya started studying earlier but achieved [enlightenment] later was that Maitreya craved fame and profit, and spent longer in mundane life. Shakyamuni, as is well known, renounced fame and profit and went [to live as an ascetic] in the forest, and did not associate with kings and nobles. We must recognize this.

The Scripture of the Transcendent Wisdom of Manjushri:

For the samadhi of unified practice, you must cast all confused thoughts into the void, and focus your mind on the real truth.

Be mindful of buddha, and continue this mindfulness from moment to moment, without ever slacking off.

In this mindfulness you will be able to see all the buddhas of the ten directions, and attain great eloquence.

The Scripture of the Concentration in which All the Buddhas of the Ten Directions are Clearly Seen:

For ninety days, do not sit or lie down. [Vow that] unless you achieve stable concentration [samadhi], you will never rest, even if your tendons break and your bones dry out.

Zhuhong's comment:

The last two passages point out that mindfulness of buddha includes all Buddhist methods. Those who practice Pure Land Buddhism must be aware of this.

The Scripture in Forty-two Chapters:

To make progress on the Path may be compared to one man doing battle with ten thousand men. He puts on his armor and sallies forth. His will may falter. He may get halfway [to the battle] and turn back. He may die in the battle. Or he may return victorious.

When people study the Path, they must strengthen their minds, and advance energetically and boldly. Not fearing what lies before them, they must destroy the multitude of demons, and attain the fruits of the Path.

Zhuhong's comment:

Those who get halfway there and retreat are the ones who circumscribe themselves and do not advance.

Those who join the battle and die are the ones who advance slightly but achieve nothing.

Those who return victorious are the ones who smash delusion and consummate the Path. The reason for their victory lies entirely in strengthening their minds and advancing energetically and boldly.

If students just go straight ahead with a single intent, they do not worry about retreating, and they do not fear death.

Hasn't it already been said? I guarantee that such a person will surely attain the Path! In the Lotus Sutra [Buddha] says: "Here and now I guarantee this thing for you: it will never be false." Since Buddha has given you a guarantee, what is there to worry about or fear?

The Scripture of the Contemplation of the Medicine King Bodhisattva:

Always be mindful of the Great Vehicle, so that your mind does not forget it. Diligently cultivate energetic progress, as if saving yourself when your head is on fire.

Zhuhong's comment:

"Diligently cultivate energetic progress, as if saving yourself when your head is on fire." These days in the monastic communities they recite [scriptures] day and night, but they recite the texts without thinking about their meaning. If you clearly understand their meaning, but do not practice the tasks [they set out], what good will it do?

The Jewel Cloud Scripture:

Use mind to focus mind, use mind to settle mind.
Mind is concentrated and unified, so there is uninterrupted progress. Mind is stabilized, so mind is always still and pure.

The Scripture on Mindfulness of the Correct Dharma:

If you cultivate practice energetically and diligently, you will be able to see the truth.
Therefore you must go into the stillness of the wilderness, and wholeheartedly practice correct mindfulness. Detach from all speech and words. Leave behind all the social intercourse of your kinfolk and old friends.

The Treatise on the Various Schools of Abhidharma Interpretation:

If I do not attain the most excellent Dharma which I have been seeking from the start, I will never stop even if my flesh and blood dry up and wither away, and only my skin and bones are left.

For the sake of energetic progress, I must endure heat and cold and hunger and thirst and poisonous snakes and stinging insects. I must endure whatever other people may do to cause my body sharp pain: I must accept it if they take my life or make me suffer or insult and revile me.

Zhuhong's comment:

"If I do not attain the most excellent Dharma which I have been seeking from the start, I will never stop." This is the same idea as the Zen saying, "If I do not smash through the koan that is my basic study, I will never rest."

The Treatise on the Yogacara Stages:

Of the six perfections, the first three, [generosity, discipline, and patience], belong to the study of discipline; [the fifth], meditation, belongs to the study of mind; and [the sixth], transcendent wisdom, belongs to the study of wisdom. Only [the fourth perfection], energetic progress, belongs to all studies.

The Treatise on the Adornment of the Great Vehicle Sutras

If you study the Path with perfect sincerity, and generate a great determination, you will surely proceed on to enlightenment.

The Treatise on Abhidharma:

In the time of Tishya Buddha [who taught both Shakyamuni and Maitreya in their earlier incarnations], there was a bodhisattva who joined his hands together and stood on one foot and for seven days and nights intoning a verse extolling the merits of the buddhas. This was better than nine eons [of practice].

Zhuhong's comment:

Observing the foregoing passages, [we see that] the Buddhist scriptures and philosophical treatises proclaim that one day of energetic progress is better than a hundred years of laziness. How true these words are!

Records of the Western Regions:

The Venerable Xie left home when he was eighty years old. A young man mocked him saying, "The task of home-leavers is either to study Zen or to recite the scriptures. By now you are already old and feeble: what progress can you make?"

When the Venerable Xie heard this, he vowed to himself, "I will never let myself lie down until I have comprehended the principles of the scriptures, cut off the desires of the triple world, and achieved supernatural powers and liberation."

From then on he studied the principles of the scriptures by day, and focused his spirit in meditative concentration by night. After three years he had realized all that he had vowed to accomplish. The people of the time venerated him, and called him 'the Venerable Xie'.

Zhuhong's comment:

An old man who is hale and hearty is enough to spur on lazy monks. It is not only eighty-year-olds who ought to try hard: even those who have reached a hundred still need to work hard to make progress.

Stories of Journeys Back from the South Seas:

Dharma teacher Shanyu recited the buddha-name whatever he was doing, and did not neglect it for a moment. If one counted [the number of times he repeated the buddha-name] with a tiny beans, they would fill two cartloads.

The Dharma Garden Forest of Pearls:

In the Tang period, the monk Zhicong of Qixia Temple dwelt to the west of the temple's reliquary. [He spent his time] either walking or sitting in meditation: he had vowed never to sit [around casually] or lie down. The eighty members of the assembly never left the temple.

Commentary on the Treatise on Contemplating Mind:

If you are not completely determined, you will not be able to succeed even if what you want to accomplish is something small—much less when you want to set aside the heavy barrier of confused perceptions, confused thoughts, and fundamental ignorance, and cross the great ocean of birth and death! If you do not work diligently, how can you mesh with the Wondrous Path?

The Yongjia Collection:

Diligently seek the Ultimate Path, unconcerned with your physical life.

Practice transcendent wisdom day and night. Diligently make progress lifetime after lifetime. Act all the time as if you are saving yourself when your head is on fire.

Guishan's "Warning Stick":

Investigate the truth of the Dharma to the end, taking enlightenment as your standard.

Zhuhong's comment:

Here "standard" means criterion and goal. [Guishan is telling you] to take enlightenment as your criterion and goal.

In the Zen school they ask, "To what point should we study Zen? What is the point where we can stop working?" Here [Guishan] says that only with great enlightenment are you finished. If you are not enlightened, you are not done.

Pure Land Repentance Vows

Whether sitting or walking, I will not let my mind scatter in confusion.   I must not think of worldly desires even for an instant.

I will not meet with outsiders to talk and joke and laugh.

I will must not put things off and create delays, or let myself indulge in sleep.

Even if I look up or down for a split second, my mindfulness [of buddha] will not be broken.

Steps to the Realm of Reality:

To redouble your efforts to urge yourself on to make energetic progress, to diligently seek without stopping: this is called the root of energetic progress.

Notes to the "Ode on Mind":

Steadfastly seek the Ultimate Path.   Day and night forget your tiredness. Do not seek outside yourself. Empty yourself of concerns and cleanse yourself of thoughts.   Sit in silence in a secret room, attune yourself and pacify your spirit.

Zhuhong's comment:

You Pure Land Buddhists should not think that you do not have to recite the buddha-name after you read these statements about not seeking outside yourself, and sitting in silence in a secret room.

You must realize that mindfulness through recitation comes from the mind, and buddha is your true self. [In reciting the buddha-name] you use your own mind to be mindful of your own true self: how could this be considered seeking outside yourself?

If you keep mindful [of buddha] by reciting [the buddha-name] without stopping, then you achieve samadhi: what could a silent secret room add to this?

Appendix:
Some Famous Koans

At an assembly on Spirit Peak, Buddha held up a flower and [his disciple] Kashyapa gave a slight smile.

Buddha said: "I have the treasury of the eye of the Correct Teaching, the wondrous mind of nirvana–I entrust it to Kashyapa."

[The bodhisattva-philosopher] Ashvaghosha said: "The mountains, rivers, and the whole earth are all established on buddha-nature, and all insights and mental powers appear from this."

Manora asked [his teacher, the bodhisattva-philosopher] Vasubandhu, "What is the enlightenment of the buddhas?"

Vasubandhu said: "It is the original nature of mind."

Liang Wudi, Emperor of South China, asked Bodhidharma, "What is the highest meaning of the holy truths?"

Bodhidharma said, "Empty, without holiness."

Zhaozhou said, "The Ultimate Path is without difficulty: just avoid picking and choosing."

Xuefeng said, "Pick up the whole world, and it's as big as a grain of rice. I throw it down before you, but being ignorant, you do not understand. I'm beating the drum to call everyone to take a look."

A monk named Huichao asked Fayan, "What is Buddha?"

Fayan said, "You are Huichao."

Huangbo said to the assembly, "All of you people are gobblers of dregs. If you go on wandering around this way, you will never have Today [the day of enlightenment]. Did you know that there are no Zen teachers in China?"

A monk came forward and asked, "What about those people all over who are regulating disciples and leading congregations?"

Huangbo said, "I didn't say there is no Zen, just that there are no teachers."

A monk asked Dongshan, "What is Buddha?" Dongshan said, "Three pounds of hemp."

A monk asked Baling, "What is philosophical analysis?" Baling said, "Piling up snow in a silver bowl."

A monk asked Yunmen, "What were the teachings [given by Buddha] for a certain period of time?"

Yunmen said, "An appropriate statement."

Emperor Suzong asked National Teacher Zhong, "What will you need a hundred years from now?"

Zhong said, "Build me a seamless monument."

Baofu and Changqing were wandering together in the mountains.

Baofu pointed and said, "Right here is the summit of the mystic peak."

Changqing said, "It is indeed: what a pity!"

Xuedou added a comment: "Today as you wander along with these guys, what are you aiming for?"

A monk asked Yunmen, "How is it when the trees wither and the leaves fall?"

Yunmen said, "Body exposed in the golden wind."

Baizhang asked Nanquan, "Is there a truth that all the sages since antiquity have never spoken for people?"

Nanquan said, "There is."

Baizhang said, "What is the truth that has never been spoken for people?"

Nanquan said, "It is not mind, it is not buddha, it is not things."

Baizhang said, "You have spoken it."

Danxia asked: "What is the true self that precedes the Empty Eon?"

Note: In Buddhist cosmology, every world-system is said to pass through eons of formation, abiding, and destruction, followed by an eon of emptiness before the formation of a new world-system.

A monk asked Dasui, "When the conflagration at the end of the age sweeps through, and the universe is destroyed, will this one be destroyed or not?"

Dasui said, "It will be destroyed."

The monk said, "If so, then we will go along with it." Dasui said, "We will go along with it."

Senior Monk Ding asked Linji, "What is the great meaning of the Buddha Dharma?"

Linji got down from the teacher's seat, held Ding tight, gave him a slap, then pushed him away. Ding just stood there.

A bystander said to Ding, "Why don't you bow?" As Ding went to bow down, suddenly he was greatly enlightened.

Panshan imparted a saying: "There is nothing in the triple world. Where will you seek mind?"
Note: the "triple world" means the world experienced as objects of desire, the world of neutral form, and the formless world of meditative states.

A monk asked Yunmen, "What is the pure Dharmakaya?"
Yunmen said, "A flowering hedge."
Note: "Dharmakaya" is the Buddha's Truth Body, the Body of Reality, Buddha as the everywhere-equal absolute reality that is the ground of being of all particular entities.

Zhaozhou asked Touzi, "How is it when the person who has died the great death returns to life?"
Touzi said, "He should not go by night: he must arrive in broad daylight."
Note: "Dying the great death" means enlightenment, the death of the false self. "Returning to life" means coming back to the world of delusion as an enlightening being to work for the salvation of deluded beings.

A monk asked Dongshan, "When hot weather and cold weather come, how can we escape?"
Dongshan said, "Why don't you go to where there is no hot and cold?"
The monk said, "What is the place where there is no hot and cold?"

Dongshan said, "When it's cold, the cold kills you, and when it's hot, the heat kills you."

Heshan imparted this saying: "Practicing and studying is called 'learning'. Being at the end of your studies is called 'being close'. Going beyond these two is real going beyond."

A monk came forward and asked, "What is real going beyond?"

Heshan said, "Knowing how to beat the drum."

The monk also asked, "What is the real truth?"

Heshan said, "Knowing how to beat the drum."

The monk asked, "When a transcendent person comes, how do you receive him?"

Heshan said, "Knowing how to beat the drum."

A monk asked Zhaozhou, "The myriad things return to one. Where does the one return to?"

Zhaozhou said, "When I was in [the town of] Qingzhou I made a cloth shirt that weighed seven pounds."

Sansheng asked Xuefeng, "What does the golden fish who has passed through the net use for food?"

Xuefeng said, "When you get out of the net, I'll tell you."

Note: The "golden fish" symbolizes our buddha-nature, our real identity, free from the net of delusion.

A monk asked Yunmen, "What is every-atom samadhi?" Yunmen said, "Food in the bowl, water in the bucket."

Note: "Samadhi" means stable meditative concentration. Every-atom means samadhi in all situations.

Yunmen took his staff and showed it to the assembly and said, "The staff changes into a dragon and has swallowed the universe. Where will we find the mountains and the rivers and the earth?"

Note: the staff represents the teaching mission of the Zen masters.

Yunmen said, "Within heaven and earth, amidst space and time, there is a jewel hidden in the mountain of form."

Every time there was a vegetarian feast, Master Jinniu would take a tub of cooked rice in front of the monks' hall, then dance around laughing out loud saying, "Little bodhisattvas, come eat!"

A monk asked Yunmen, "What is talk that transcends the buddhas and ancestral teachers?"

Yunmen said, "Cake."

A monk asked Zhaozhou, "Does a newborn infant have intellectual consciousness or not?"

Zhaozhou said, "[It's like] a ball tossed on a swift-flowing stream."

Yunmen said, "Every person has a light. But when they look at it, it does not appear, and they are dark and dim. What is everyone's light?"

Zhaozhou said, "A plaster buddha does not pass through water. A metal buddha does not pass through a smelter. A wooden buddha does not pass through fire."

A monk asked Zhaozhou, "Does a dog have buddha-nature or not?"

Zhaozhou said, "No."

Xiangyan said, "Suppose a person is hanging from a tree branch by his teeth. Someone beneath the tree asks the meaning of Zen. If the person in the tree does not answer, he is spurning the question. If he does answer, he loses his life. How should he reply?"

A monk said to Zhaozhou, "I have just entered the Zen community and I request you to instruct me, Master."

Zhaozhou said, "Have you eaten yet or not?"

The monk said, "I have."

Zhaozhou said, "Then go wash your bowl."

Every day Master Ruiyan would call to himself, "Boss!" Then he would answer himself, "Yes?" Then he would say, "Wake up!" "I will" "From now on, don't fall for other people's deceptions." "I won't, I won't."

The National Teacher called his attendant three times, and three times the attendant answered.

The National Teacher said, "I had thought that I was turning my back on you, but actually it is you who are turning your back on me."

When a monk asked him, "What is Buddha?" Yunmen said, "A dry piece of shit"

Yangshan dreamed that he went to Maitreya Buddha's place and occupied the third seat in the assembly. A venerable one pounded the gavel and said,

"Today the one in the third seat will expound the Dharma."

Yangshan got up, pounded the gavel, and said, "The Dharma of the Great Vehicle is beyond all the permutations of affirmation and denial. Listen carefully!"
Note: Maitreya is the future buddha.

Before a vegetarian feast was to take place, some monks came to study with Fayan. Fayan pointed to the screen, and two monks went at the same time to roll it up.

Fayan said, "One gains, one loses."

The wind was making the temple flag flutter. There were two monks arguing. One said the flag was moving. One said the wind was moving. They argued back and forth without reaching the truth.

The Sixth Patriarch said to them, "It is not the wind moving, and it is not the flag moving. It is your minds that are moving." The two monks were startled.

When Damei asked him, "What is Buddha?" Mazu said, "Mind itself is Buddha."

Nanquan said, "Mind is not Buddha, wisdom is not the Path."

Wuzu asked a monk, "When the soul of a pretty woman has departed, what is the true person?"

Wuzu said, "When you meet a person who has consummated the Path, do not answer him with words or silence. Tell me, with what do you reply to him?"

A monk asked, "What is the meaning of coming from the West?"

Zhaozhou said, "The cypress tree in the garden."

Note: According to tradition, Bodhidharma, the First Patriarch of Zen in China, came from India ("the West") to China to transmit the Zen message in person .

In ancient times, Manjushri came to a conclave of buddhas. When all the buddhas returned to their own abodes, a woman remained in samadhi near the seat of Shakyamuni Buddha.

Manjushri asked Shakyamuni, "How is it that a woman can approach your seat, but I cannot."

Shakyamuni told Manjushri, "Arouse her from her samadhi, and ask her."

Manjushri walked around the woman three times and snapped his fingers. Then he transported her up to heaven. He used all his supernatural powers, but could not bring her out of samadhi.

Shakyamuni said, "Even a hundred thousand Manjushris could not bring this woman out of samadhi. But twelve hundred million worlds below us, there is a bodhisattva called 'Netted Light' who can bring her out of samadhi."

That very instant, 'Netted Light' popped up out of the ground and bowed to Shakyamuni. Shakyamuni gave a command, and 'Netted Light' went up to the woman and snapped his fingers once. At that the woman came out of her samadhi.

Note: Manjushri is the transhistorical bodhisattva who represents transcendent wisdom.

Fayan of East Mountain said, "Shakyamuni Buddha and Maitreya Buddha are *his* slaves: who is *he?*"

Master Shishuang said, "How can you advance from the top of a hundred foot pole?"

Another ancient worthy said, "Although a person sitting at the top of a hundred foot pole has gained entry [into the Path], this is not yet the Real. From the top of a hundred foot pole, you must take a step forward, and manifest the whole body in all the worlds of the ten directions."

Note: Being at the top of a hundred foot pole represents a peak of meditative concentration and unity.

Master Yue of Tushita Temple set three barriers for students:

"You push aside the weeds [of crude delusion] to study the mystery, aiming to see your real nature. Where is your real nature right now?"

"Only when you recognize your own real nature do you escape from birth and death. When the light in your eyes falls [and your physical death is at hand], how will you escape?"

"When you have escaped from birth and death, you know where you are going to. When the four elements [that join to form your physical body] disperse, where do you go?"

A monk asked Qianfeng, "[For Buddha]. the Lord of the ten directions, [there is] one single road through the gate of nirvana. Where does the road start?"

Qianfeng picked up his staff, drew a line on the ground with it, and said, "Right here."

One day the World Honored One [Buddha] sat in the teacher's seat.

Manjushri pounded the gavel and said, "Carefully observe the teaching of the King of the Dharma: the teaching of the King of the Dharma is like this."

Then the World Honored One left the seat.

A king in eastern India invited Prajnatara, the Twenty-Seventh Patriarch [of Zen in India] to a vegetarian feast. The king asked him, "Why don't you recite sutras?"

Prajnatara said, "As I breathe in, I do not dwell in form, sensation, perception, motivational synthesis or consciousness, or in the realms of sense faculties and sense objects. As I breathe out, I do not become involved with the myriad objects. I am always reciting this sutra, and I have done so hundreds and thousands and millions of times."

Once when the World Honored One was out walking with a large group of companions, he pointed to the ground with his hand and said, "A temple should be built here."

Indra [the king of the gods] took a blade of grass and stuck it in the ground and said, "The temple has been built."

The World Honored One smiled.

A monk asked Qingyuan, "What is the great meaning of the Buddha Dharma?"

Qingyuan said, "What is the price of rice in [the city of] Luling?"

A monk asked Zhaozhou, "Does a dog have buddha-nature or not?"

Zhaozhou said, "It does."

The monk said, "Since it does, when then does it rush into this skin bag?"

Zhaozhou said, "It knows, but deliberately transgresses."

A monk asked Yunmen, "If you do not arouse a single thought, is there still any fault or not?"

Yunmen said, "Mount Sumeru."

Note: Mount Sumeru in Buddhist cosmology is a colossal polar mountain at the center of the world. In Zen parlance it sometimes stands for phenomenal reality as a whole.

Yunmen said, "When the ancient buddhas and the pillar here intersect, what level of mind is it?"

The assembly said nothing.

Yunmen answered for them, "Clouds arise on South Mountain, rain falls on North Mountain."

Linji told the assembly, "There is a true person without position going in and out through your faces. Those of you [who are at the stage] of the first aspiration [for enlightenment], who have not yet witnessed it, look, look!"

Luoshan asked Yantou, "How is it when arising and extinction take place ceaselessly?"

Yantou grunted in rebuke and said, "Who is it that is arising and becoming extinct?"

Yanyang asked Zhaozhou, "How is it when I don't bring a single thing?"

Zhaozhou said, "Put it down."

Yanyang said, "I am not bringing a single thing: put what down?"

Zhaozhou said, "Then pick it up."

The Huayan Sutra says that when Shakyamuni Buddha was first enlightened he said: "Today I see that all sentient beings fully possess the qualities of the Tathagatas' wisdom. But because of false thoughts and attachments, they do not experience it."

Shakyamuni Buddha realized enlightenment upon seeing the morning star. He said: "All sentient beings on earth and I attain enlightenment together at the same time."

Notes

1. The three most famous classic koan collections have been translated into English. These are *The Blue Cliff Record* (translated by Thomas Cleary & J. C. Cleary), and the *Book of Equanimity* and the *Gateless Barrier* (translated by Thomas Cleary).

2. An example of this kind of decoding is found in J. C. Cleary, *A Tune Beyond the Clouds* (Asian Humanities Press, 1991).

3. See J. C. Cleary, *Worldly Wisdom* (Shambhala, 1991) for translated teachings of Buddhist-influenced Confucians.